Shakespeare on Love

Shakespeare on Love:
The Sonnets and Plays in Relation to Plato's Symposium, Alchemy, Christianity and Renaissance Neo-Platonism

By

Ronald Gray
Fellow of Emmanuel College
Cambridge University

**CAMBRIDGE
SCHOLARS**
PUBLISHING

Shakespeare on Love:
The Sonnets and Plays in Relation to Plato's Symposium, Alchemy, Christianity
and Renaissance Neo-Platonism,
by Ronald Gray

This book first published 2011

Cambridge Scholars Publishing

12 Back Chapman Street, Newcastle upon Tyne, NE6 2XX, UK

British Library Cataloguing in Publication Data
A catalogue record for this book is available from the British Library

ISBN (10): 1-4438-2711-8, ISBN (13): 978-1-4438-2711-9

FOR DOROTHY

FROM REVIEWS OF BOOKS
BY RONALD GRAY

Goethe the Alchemist: 'This book is a major contribution to Goethe Studies' (W.H. Bruford, Professor of German, Cambridge University).
Brecht: 'Mr Gray's essay on Brecht seems to me the best criticism of the plays available in English ... a positive relief after the endless circling and the chatter of Brecht selling' (Raymond Williams, Professor of English, Cambridge University).
Kafka's Castle: 'This is a most impressive and convincing investigation of Kafka's novel and just the sort of study that needed to be written at the present moment ... One would gladly dispense with much of the voluminous literature (on Kafka) in return for more from Dr Gray' (W. Lucas, Professor of German, Manchester University).
Franz Kafka. Carefully written and researched, aware of secondary literature, novel in some aspects but not opinionated, this book will truly facilitate the study of this enigmatic writer for non-German readers. Anyone who desires a guide in his searchings for Kafka's meaning will do well to read this book from cover to cover. Much that is said about Kafka's perfection, about his battle with his sense of degradation, about what ultimately inspired Kafka's fiction, has not been said better. (Anon. in *Choice*.)
Introduction to German Poetry: Mr Gray's book is one of those that help more than they seem to promise. It applies, in the happiest manner, something like I.A. Richard's *Practical Criticism* to the reading of German poetry, and makes a stimulating vade-mecum. Never bludgeoning, never condescending, Mr Gray persuades the student by asking many pertinent questions, to read closely, think clearly and develop his sensitivity' (Anon, *Times Educational Supplement*).
Goethe: A Critical Introduction: '... this readable and intelligent book .... Possibly cavils a little too much ... Even so, it is the best of its kind available to English readers, and rather better than so reserved a commendation suggests' (D.J. Enright, in *The Listener*).
Poems of Goethe: 'Dr Gray's interpretations are as always based on sound scholarship, stimulating, indeed provocative and happily free from jargon ... Dr Gray is particularly good at detecting artificiality, pretentiousness and coyness' (W.E. Yuill, Professor of German, Nottingham University).

TABLE OF CONTENTS

BY THE SAME AUTHOR

1952   *Goethe the Alchemist. A study of alchemical symbolism in Goethe's literary and scientific works* (Cambridge University Press).

1956   *Kafka's Castle* (C.U.P.)

1961   *Brecht* (Oliver and Boyd)

1962   *The Twentieth Century Views Kafka. A Collection of Critical Essays)* (ed.) (Prentice-Hall).

1965   *An Introduction to German Poetry* (C.U.P.). Revised publication as *German Poetry. A Guide to Free Appreciation* 1976 (C.U.P.)

1966   *Poems of Goethe. A Selection with Introduction and Notes* (C.U.P.).

1967   *The German Tradition in Literature 1871-1945* (C.U.P.)

1967   *Goethe. A Critical Introduction* (C.U.P.).

1976   *Brecht the Dramatist* (C.U.P.)

1973   *Franz Kafka* (C.U.P.).

2006   'Will in the Universe. Shakespeare's Sonnets and Plato's *Symposium* and Alchemy and Renaissance Neo-Platonism', *Shakespeare Survey 59* (C.U.P.), pp.225-238.

Contributions to *Modern Language Review, The Times Literary Supplement, The Listener, The Guardian, The Daily Telegraph, The New Statesman, German Life and Letters, Cambridge Quarterly, The Gadfly, The Human World, The New Humanist,* etc.

PROLOGUE

Contradictions and stark contrasts abound in the Sonnets as in the plays. Malvolio's absurd compliance to what he believes to be Olivia's wishes are a travesty of the Sonnets poet's devotion. The poet declares he is his lover's adversary and advocate. The poet's mistress can do no wrong: 'all my best doth worship thy defect'. For the witches' chorus in *Macbeth* 'fair is foul and foul is fair'. The two lovers in *The Phoenix and the Turtle* are 'two distincts, division none', like the Sonnets poet and his lover, who is both real and a fusion of two sexes ('for a woman wert thou first created'). The apparently mystical union in Sonnet 33 is echoed in Bottom the Weaver's garbled version of St Paul's account of ecstasy. The tragic ending of *Romeo and Juliet* has exactly the same sequence of events as the hilarious farce of Pyramus and Thisbe, performed by Bottom's company.

In the study that follows these and other contrasts and contradictions are related to the universal vision of love in Plato's *Symposium* and in Renaissance neo-Platonism and alchemy.

PREFACE

This book expands the article which was published in 2006 in *Shakespeare Survey 59* (Cambridge University Press), entitled 'Will in the Universe: Shakespeare's Sonnets, Plato's *Symposium*, Alchemy and Renaissance Neoplatonism'. It includes also a chapter on 'The Muse', a chapter on 'A Lover's Complaint', arguing for Shakespeare's authorship of this poem, and one on 'Varied Perceptions of Philosophies of Opposites', considering Shakespeare's place in a tradition beginning with Heraclitus and ending with T.S. Eliot. 'Dante and Shakespeare' concludes.

William Empson's study of ambiguities, still engaging after eighty years, is broadly similar to my own thesis, although Empson treats no passages in Shakespeare that I treat, and *vice-versa*. His concern is for the most part with verbal analysis, puns, grammar, punctuation, with ambiguities arising from these, treating mostly short extracts. Only in the last chapter but one does he deal with contradicting opposites, and here he touches on mysticism, as I do, as well as Freud. He is not concerned with the contraries in regard to love. I hope readers will find us complementary, nevertheless, though I am no match for Empson's urbanity and wit.

Mahood's study of word-play again mentions none of the passages I quote, but may also be seen as a complement to my own, which ranges more widely than Mahood's in comparing single Sonnets with other Sonnets, Sonnets with plays, plays with plays, and includes some indications of a European background in both poetry and philosophy against which Shakespeare's achievements can be seen. Mahood is, like Empson, not concerned with love.

A.D. Nuttall's recent work on *Shakespeare the Thinker* (2007) seemed likely at first to have interpreted in a way similar to my own. But although Professor Nuttall interprets *Measure for Measure* in terms of a paradoxical heresy, it does not deal with alchemy, or Plato or the neo-Platonists, but merely one of a great variety of interpretations of dialectical philosophies which I outline in a final chapter. Alchemy, however, was certainly known to Shakespeare in all its practical and symbolical meanings, whereas he is more likely not to have heard of Gnosticism in any form. Noel Cobb's study of secret alchemy at the heart of *The Tempest* has more to do with the psychological ideas of C.G. Jung than with the play.

Much closer to my own argument is Robert Grudin in his *Mighty Opposites, Shakespeare and Renaissance Contrariety* (1979) which is concerned, as I am, with the philosophy of polarity in Renaissance thinkers. We differ, for example, as regards the paradox in Castiglione's view that without evil 'there would be no real goodness', that 'goodness necessitates evil' (p.20), which I do not find, as Grudin does, in relation to *King Lear* and *Measure for Measure*. Michael McCanles' *Dialectical Criticism and Renaissance Literature* (1975) is also concerned with polar opposites, but McCanles confines himself to discussing 'The Dialectic of Right and Power in Eight Plays of Shakespeare'. This is mainly political, outside my own field of interest. McCanles also writes about Donne, Herbert, Marvell and *Paradise Lost* as part of the same dialectical traditions, affording much less space to Shakespeare in particular. I often felt an affinity with G. Wilson Knight's views, although I see Nietzsche as only one of many writers in the same broad tradition. I stress that the alchemical and Platonist aspects present a wholly different scenario, which affects also my view of Helen Vendler's distinguished *Art of Shakespeare's Sonnets*, and Stephen Greenblatt's *Will in the World*.

There is no mention of interpretations of the Sonnets in relation to alchemy in Rollins' Variorum Edition of 1944, apart from the textual editing of 'alcumy', and little since that date.[1] Margaret Healy's *Shakespeare, Alchemy and the Creative Imagination* was announced for 2011 by C.U.P. at a time when the present book was being corrected in proof.

The great knowledge of occultist and Rosicrucian philosophies, both of them related to alchemy, in the works of Frances Yates, gave little insight into the influence of alchemy itself or of Plato on Shakespeare. Her chief work on Shakespeare, *Shakespeare's Last Plays. A New Approach*, she summarized as showing Shakespeare's great creations – Hamlet, Lear, Prospero belonging to the last stage of 'Renaissance occultist philosophy', struggling in the throes of the reaction.

James Schiffer's Introduction, 'Reading New Life into Shakespeare's Sonnets', to the critical essays on the Sonnets, edited by him, provides a survey that adds accounts of most of the work of all kinds done since Rollins' time, as well as of a few earlier pieces. (The internet bears witness to a very large increase in interest in alchemy generally in recent times.)

David Schalkwyk's *Speech and Performance in Shakespeare's Sonnets and Plays* (2002) treats the connection between the Sonnets and plays in a way entirely different from my own, concerning itself with philosophical

[1] See Schiffer.

issues related to Wittgenstein and J.L. Austin. His *Shakespeare, Love and Service*, although treating the interaction of love and service in the Sonnets and plays, also approaches them differently. Joel Fineman's *Shakespeare's Perjured Eye: The Invention of Poetic Subjectivity in the Sonnets*, widely influential, is also philosophical and linguistic in its approach, in the field of studies by Lacan and de Saussure.

I am very much indebted to friends, especially Dorothy Sturley, and colleagues, some of whom have been aware of my interests for the twenty-eight years since I retired. I thank most cordially Professor John Kerrigan, and Professors Colin Burrow and Katherine Duncan-Jones, for expert critical comment at a later stage. I thank also Fellows of Emmanuel College, the late Professor Derek Brewer, Professors Peter Burke and Geoffrey Hill, Dr John Harvey and Dr Christopher Burlinson, the Rev. Don Cupitt, as well as Dr Leo Salingar, Dr Douglas Cook, Dr Bernard Brown and Mr John Martin, for their encouragement at many stages in the book's development. Members of the University of the Third Age in Cambridge participated in discussions of the Sonnets over several years, which were also of great help to me. Professor W.E. Yates encouraged me to write about the Austrian dramatist Grillparzer.[2] My knowledge of the plays was helped by many Shakespearean discussions I hosted under the chairmanship of Harold Mason and by my years as Senior Treasurer of Cambridge University Marlowe Dramatic Society. Some of the present book repeats arguments I used in the article in *Shakespeare Survey 59*.

I warmly thank my daughter Sue, and her husband Professor Robin Perutz, Vivien Perutz, my son Professor John Gray and his late wife Professor Jean Rudduck.

I am most grateful to Mrs Linda Allen who has typed my many revisions year after year with great accuracy and patience with my handwriting.

---

[2] See 'Grillparzer and Shakespeare' in *Grillparzer und die europäische Tradition*, edd. Alex Stillmark, W.E. Yates, Fred Wagner, Vienna 1987.

CHAPTER ONE

CONTRARIES AND COINCIDENCES

Let me not to the marriage of true mindes
Admit impediments, love is not love
Which alters when it alteration findes,
Or bends with the remover to remove.
O no, it is an ever fixed marke
That lookes on tempests and is never shaken;
It is the star to every wandring barke,
Whose worths unknowne, although his higth be taken.
Lov's not Times foole, though rosie lips and cheeks
Within his bending sickles compasse come,
Love alters not with his breefe hours and weekes,
But beares it out even to the edge of doome;
    If this be error and upon me proved,
    I never writ, nor no man ever loved.

This is probably the best known of all the Sonnets, the word
'impediment' echoing the marriage ceremony in the Book of Common
Prayer, where the priest asks whether there is any reason why the bridal
couple should not be married. Other Christian parallels may also come to
mind, especially St Paul's famous words on Charity (or Agapé),
contrasting with Eros: Charity (Geneva Bible: Love):[1]

> suffereth long, and is kind [bountiful], ...envieth not, ... vaunteth not
> itself ... seeketh not her own, is not easily provoked [not provoked to
> anger], thinketh no evil, rejoiceth not in iniquity, but rejoiceth in the truth.
> (I *Cor.* 13.4-6)

Shakespeare certainly knew these lines, as he also must have known the
Song of Solomon in the Old Testament:

---

[1] Quotations from the Geneva Bible of 1584 are given only if significantly
different from the Authorised Version.

> many waters cannot quench love,
> Neither can the floods drown it.
> (*S. of S.* 7.7.)

Sonnets 153 and 154 allude to these verses, with the assertion that 'the holie fire of love' cannot be put out by any bath, and that 'Loves fire heates water, water cooles not love'. The *Song of Solomon* is, however, an erotic poem, and the love it speaks of is not essentially like St Paul's. Shakespeare often combines both.

There are also moments in both the Sonnets and the plays where a lover is inspired more by Jesus's love that turns the other cheek, and does not resist evil (*Matt.* 5.39 and 44).. Shakespeare inherits this along with Agapé and Eros, a part of a long tradition that stretches back to pagan sources as much as to Christian and Judaic ones, as he suggests in the Sonnet immediately following 116, where he says he has 'frequent binne with unknown mindes' (117.3). If the man whose 'great deserts' the poet has failed to repay, the man whose 'deare purchas'd right' (117.5-6) he has ignored, is meant to recall Christ, and there are reasons, to be explored later, for thinking he does, the poet is confessing that he has been in the habit of reading unorthodox authors, and even perhaps adopting their ideas. He has

> hoisted sayle to al the windes
> Which should transport me farthest from your sight.
> (117.7-8)

Something similar is suggested already in the couplet of 116, where the poet concedes that what he has just said about love may be 'error', as though it were not in accord with some official statement of doctrine, which might be 'proved' [tested] as though by some Inquisition. In fact he has not been entirely orthodox, for all the resemblance to St Paul. The marriage he speaks of in 116 is not necessarily one of a man and a woman: it is rather a marriage of true minds, which may be the minds of a man and a woman, or of two male or two female lovers. The unknown writer in whom such a love is celebrated could well be Plato, and we may now turn to see what Shakespeare knew of him, and how much it inspired him. Plato's works, scarcely known in Europe before the late fifteenth century when they were translated into Latin by Marsilio Ficino, brought new perceptions of religion to the whole Western world. His *Symposium* especially made a great impact. Spenser admired it, and there is in fact, as will appear, a passage in the *Symposium* which Shakespeare knew and imitated fairly closely.

At the climax of the discussion of love in its various forms, Socrates relates how he was told by a wise woman called Diotima about a vision of universal love that might be attained by a man loving first one, then many men, finally bursting forth as 'a wondrous vision which is the very soul of the beauty he has so long toiled for' (para.211). This is for Socrates, as Plato portrays him, so convincing that he tries to bring others to realise it also. 'Every man of us should worship the god of Love, ... all my life I shall pay the power and the might of Love such homage as I can' (para.211).

Socrates and St Paul are alike, yet not alike. Both celebrate Love, but for Socrates this means love of Beauty, inspired by Eros, while for St Paul beauty is never explicitly mentioned, and Eros is a hindrance. It is better to marry than to burn with passion (I *Cor.* 7.9). Jesus speaks with apparent approval of men who make themselves eunuchs for the kingdom of heaven's sake (*Matthew* 19.12), and the history of Christianity until recently has on the whole looked at celibacy as preferable to marriage. Shakespeare in the first seventeen Sonnets is decidedly in favour of beauty as the fruit of sexual desire.

Sonnet 1 announces a theme that runs through all the Sonnets up to number 17: that a young man should do all he can to beget a child. It may be, it has been thought, that Shakespeare was commissioned by a mother whose son was not inclined to marry, to write encouraging him. But even if that is so, it does not reveal in what spirit Shakespeare writes. He is in love with the young man, though quite capable of addressing him with scorn as well as adoration, and the whole point of these Sonnets is the necessity not to promote some family estate, but to make sure Beauty remains throughout generation after generation. Marriage, as distinct from having children, is never really mentioned. There are many women, the poet tells the man, who would be glad to help.

The aim is that 'beauties Rose might never die (1.2), as though each new child perpetuated the beauty of its father, maintaining it in existence. *Rose* is printed in italics in the Quarto version of 1609 (the only version published in Shakespeare's lifetime, which I shall quote throughout rather than any edited version). This may not matter – the compositors of that time could be wayward, and print italics where none was intended. The word does, however, suggest the symbolical significance of, for example, the *Roman de la Rose*, translated by Chaucer, where the Rose is a flower at the centre of the garden of Love, and the rose of antiquity, sacred to Venus, as portrayed in Renaissance and later art.[2]

---

[2] James Hall, *Dictionary of Subject and Symbols in Art*, John Murray, 1974, rev.ed., 1979, p.268.

The child possessing this beauty is expected to resemble its parent completely — 'thou art thy mothers glasse [mirror], and she in thee calls backe the lovely Aprill of her prime' (3.9-10), and this we must accept for the poem's sake. Bernard Shaw was right when he replied to a woman who proposed marriage 'What if the child inherits my body and your brains?'[3] In fact the genealogical issue is less relevant than the symbolical, for the inheritance is that of a 'summe of summes' (4.8), a substance rather than a shadow (5.14), a gift of nature that should be cherished (11.12), truth and beauty combined (14.11). It is even a kind of distillation (5.8), though not an alchemical one This is not to say that the young man is not a mortal like anyone else. To maintain his beauty is even equivalent, the poet argues, to maintaining his virtue to confront a kind of Last Judgment: What will he say, the poet asks, if he is ever challenged in old age to show what has become of the beauty he had in his youth, and has no child to show he has preserved it (2.4-12)? What 'acceptable *Audit* can he leave' (4.12). This unusual combination of the Christian Day of Judgment with the pagan worship of Beauty is worth noting in the Sonnets following 17. Christianity and pagan religion momentarily combine.

In Sonnet 18 the sequence reaches an unexpected conclusion. Sonnet 17 had ended with the reply the young man might make if the beauty ascribed to him by the poet were to be doubted and were regarded as mere hyperbole. If he had a child, its beauty would complement that of the poems:

> But were some childe of yours alive that time,
> You should live twise in it, and in my rime.
> (17.13-14)

It would do more than complement, Sonnet 18 now argues, or rather announces with swelling grandeur:

> But thy eternall Sommer shall not fade
> Nor loose possession of that faire thou ow'st, [ownest]
> Nor shall death brag thou wanderst in his shade,
> When in eternall lines to time thou grow'st
> (18.9-12)

The 'eternall lines' have a double sense: they are both the lines of the poem and the lines of descent, through which beauty is preserved from one

[3] Justin Wintle and Richard Herrin, *The Penguin Concise Biographical Quotations*, Penguin Books, 1981, p.558 (quoting Hesketh Pearson, *Bernard Shaw. His Life and Personality*).

generation to another — and this is not merely a pun. The poet has begun to see that beauty is not simply a matter of facial or bodily form, but can be equally present in poetry. And to appreciate this we need to consider what the *Symposium* has to say.

Young men are lying round a table enjoying a banquet and relating their ideas about love. It is always about love between men, as it is in many of the Sonnets, or the love of men for beautiful boys. Aristophanes the writer of comedies tells a story of a time when there was a race of human beings who were of both male and female gender, and who assaulted Zeus on Mount Olympus, only to be sliced in half as 'one slices an apple' and set down each with either male or female genitals. Love, he announces, is the everlasting quest for the other half. Shakespeare evidently knew of this, for in *Twelfth Night* he gives a speech to Antonio, seeing for the first time Viola with her brother, her identical twin, saying:

How have you made division of yourself?
An apple cleft in two is not more twin
Than these two creatures.
(*T.N.* 5.1.221-2)

It could be, of course, that he had only heard of Aristophanes' story from Ben Jonson or some other learned friend. His knowledge of the climax of the speeches is another matter. When it is the turn of Socrates to speak he describes his encounter with Diotima, from whom he learned how a lover 'will fall in love with the beauty of an individual body', and how he must then consider 'how nearly related the beauty of one body is to the beauty of any other', and then 'set himself to be the lover of every lovely body'. From this the lover will see that 'the beauties of the body are nothing to the beauties of the soul … and from this he will be led to contemplate the beauty of laws and institutions' (para.210). Shakespeare seems to have been inspired by this passage when he wrote, as we just saw, that the beauty of his verse and the beauty of the child-to-be were one and the same. He does not take the further steps described by Diotima, seeing beauty in institutions. But he is very likely to have been influenced by her when he wrote of his lover's presence everywhere.

Speake of the spring, and foyzon [harvest] of the yeare,
The one doth shadow of your beautie show.
The other as your bountie doth appeare,
And you *in every blessed* shape we know.
In *all externall grace* you have some part …
(53.9-13)

The beauty of nature is still only a shadow of the man's. (Here, like many other poets of his time, Shakespeare is thinking of Plato's myth of the Cave, *Republic*, book 7 in which men take the shadows they see on the wall of the cave where they are imprisoned for the reality which exists in an ideal world unknown to them.) Similarly, the poet sees the beauty of the violet, the lily and the rose as 'stolen' from his lover (99.1-14). They were 'but figures of delight', 'Drawne after you, you *patterne* [italics inserted] of all those'; the poet has only the 'shaddow' and must be contented (98.12-14). As in Plato's philosophy of ideals, the true form of things is beyond our ken, but we may see in reality an imitation of the pattern.

There are difficulties in Plato's thought here. In the myth of the Cave the imprisoned men see only shadows. This is not the same as imitations from a pattern, which can still afford, as Shakespeare says, 'delight'. This has to be borne in mind in other passages, where the young man somehow seems to be an ideal figure, not a shadow.

Easily the most far-reaching part of the *Symposium* is the section in which Diotima reveals the climax of the lover's progress.

And now, Socrates, there bursts upon him that wondrous vision which is the very soul of the beauty he has toiled so long for. It is an everlasting loveliness which neither comes nor goes, which neither flowers nor fades … subsisting of itself and by itself in an eternal oneness; while every lovely thing partakes of in such sort that, however much the parts may wax and wane, it will be neither more nor less, but still the same individual whole. (para.211)

Shakespeare reflects the 'eternal oneness', of which Diotima speaks, in Sonnet 84: 'which can say more, Than this rich praise, that you alone, are you' (84.1-2). In 124, however, he adopts much more of her description:

Yf my deare love were but the childe of state,
It might for fortunes basterd be unfathered,
As subject to times love, or to times hate,
Weeds among weeds, or flowers with flowers gatherd.
No it was buylded far from accident,
It suffers not in smilinge pomp, nor falls
Under the blow of thralled discontent,
Whereto th'inviting time our fashion calls:
It feares not policy, that *Hereticke*,
Which workes on leases of short numbred howers,
But all alone stands hugely pollitick,
That it nor growes with heat nor drownes with showres.

'All alone': Shakespeare, although he uses these words, does not commit himself to them as Plotinus did. He more probably put the passage from Plato into verse without considering every detail. For the most famous of the neo-Platonists, 'a liberation from all terrene concerns', a life unaccompanied with human pleasures, and, in his famous words 'a flight of the alone to the alone' was a supreme good.[4] Shakespeare's concerns were very much with human pleasures. His love is, he continues, nevertheless not subject to the vagaries of time, is 'not Times foole' (116.9) but exists far from the accidentals, in the philosophical sense of a property of a thing which is not essential to its nature, but is, like Plato's ideal world, 'an everlasting loveliness', the world outside the shadows, in short an 'ever fixed marke' (116.9), not shaken by tempests, or by events in time. Rebellion and the flattery of courts are unknown to it. It does not fear policy's adaptability to changing circumstances, but stands all alone, as in Diotima's words: 'subsisting of itself and by itself in an eternal oneness'. It is 'hugely pollitick': adapted to all circumstances, rather than seeking one course or another.[5] It is not a heretic, who adopts one aspect of a religion, in contrast to the Church, which claims to comprehend the whole. It is unchanging: neither heat nor rain alters it, as Diotima also says 'it neither comes nor goes, flowers nor fades'.[6]

The poet adopts this ideal love as his own. But he does not speak of any long pilgrimage such as Diotima describes, and may simply have adopted her description as satisfying his ambition. He may not have experienced any vision. Yet the question still remains, whether he did so, in the light of some other Sonnets to which I now turn. Not only St Paul is concerned with absolute love: many other strands of thought were current in the sixteenth century, adding various new features, all converging on one another in various ways. First comes alchemy, the search for a power to transmute base metals into gold.

Alchemy began with attempts at gilding naturally or artificially for purposes of decoration. From Egypt it travelled through Arab culture to Europe in the twelfth or thirteenth century, and was seen as a means of not merely decorating with gold but making it out of so-called base metals. An alchemist called Nicholas Flamel was said to have made a huge fortune. But there was a catch. To achieve so much you needed a Philosophers' Stone, *lapis philosophorum*, and if you read alchemical works you would discover the necessary ingredients, Mercury and Sulphur – not, however,

---

[4] Mead, p.322.
[5] Evans glosses 'something' immensely, vastly prudent or sagacious, unaltered. OUP edition of the Sonnets, *The New Cambridge Shakespeare*, 1996, p.238.
[6] The couplet of 124 is obscure and would take too long to expound.

the substances usually known by that name, but the 'philosophical' kind, and what these were would be revealed in due course. Nobody was ever again successful – if Flamel himself ever was. When books began to be printed they would be illustrated with dragons, basilisks, a child blazing with light, a serpent biting its tail, and often a man and a woman, both with wings, engaged in intercourse. Bringing the metals to this point by means of heating them in a chemical retort alchemists spent fruitless hours in front of dirty furnaces with great risk of fires breaking out. Yet despite the failures, they continued for at least three hundred years. Swindlers like Subtle and Surly in Ben Jonson's play *The Alchemist* profited by promising the gullible endless means of producing gold. Shakespeare was well aware of the fruitlessness of the ancient pursuit. Timon of Athens, striking a poet, mocks him with an impossibility: 'You are an alchemist. Make gold of that!' (*Timon of Athens* 5.1.114). Yet alchemical symbols are often used poetically in the Sonnets as well as in the plays. On the other hand, Isaac Newton was, even in the late seventeenth and early eighteenth centuries, so persuaded that there must be some seriousness behind all this nonsense, that he copied out reams and reams of alchemical literature, being convinced, probably, that having been granted by Providence his great scientific discoveries, the Philosophers' Stone must also come his way.

There was a serious side. Even Jonson's Surly objected that the Stone requires:

A pious, holy and religious man,
One free from mortal sin, a very virgin.
(*The Alchemist* 2.2.97-8)

There is in fact a resemblance between the achieving of the Stone and Diotoma's revelation of universal love. For a mystic like the self-educated Silesian cobbler, Jakob Boehme, almost an exact contemporary of Shakespeare, alchemical language suited his mystical vision completely. For him Sulphur was the Wrath, and Mercury the Love or Mercy of God, while the union of the two, so often shown as a sexual intercourse, was connected with the female Shekinah of the Jewish Kabbala, who was a mirror-image of God. 'The true name of the Stone', Basil Valentine declared, was 'according to temporal understanding, called ALL IN ALL.[7] Oswald Croll, a follower of Paracelsus, writes that the alchemists

---

[7] Basil Valentine, *Von dem grossen Stein der Uhralten*, Franckenhausen 1602, p.24. Translation of quoted passage by R. Gray.

'leave themselves, and totally go out from themselves …' seeking the 'one MIND which is above every MIND'. They look for 'the intimate vision of God … a foretaste of the Celestial country'.[8]

It is conceivable that this foretaste had somehow survived from the vision of universal love in the *Symposium*. The two opposites, Sulphur and Mercury, can be seen as the alchemical inheritance of the hermaphrodites in Aristophanes' fable – though beings combining male and female can be found in many other cultures. The 'chemical marriage' reflects the sexual union, so often spoken of in the writings of mystics like St Teresa of Avila and St John of the Cross, also has an unexpected Platonic parallel, for Diotima tells Socrates that 'to love is to bring forth upon the beautiful, *both in body* and soul' (para.206. Italics added). Platonic love, usually meaning a love without erotic attraction, is at least in this one place, more akin to mystical love, often described as a mystic *marriage*.

Another parallel is with Renaissance neo-Platonism, which puts in intellectual form what alchemists put in pictures and symbols. Nicholas of Cusa, a German who was highly regarded by Florentine neo-Platonists, introduced the expression *coincidentia oppositorum*, not so much as including male and female, but as the state of the world as we know it, a continual opposition of all kinds, and the coincidence of all such opposites in God. It is easy to see the alchemical parallel here, but it reappears in Hegel's polarities, progression from one pair of opposites to a fusion of both, and a renewed opposition followed again by fusion.[9] In fact the symbolism of male and female can create infinite pairs, if one accepts the premise that they are as inclusive as is claimed, for example, by Goethe, who writes that we speak of a 'here' and a 'there', 'above' and 'below', 'before' and 'after', 'activity' and 'passivity', 'male and female'.[10]

There is often a resemblance in this form of neo-Platonism to Petrarchism, with which Shakespeare was familiar. The sonnet form itself is strongly influenced by Petrarch, and so are the use of antithesis, oxymoron and other combinations of opposites. Mercutio mocks Romeo as a would-be Petrarch (*R and J*, 2.4.41), and Romeo offers confirmation of this when he reels off a Petrarchan list: "O heavy lightness, serious vanity, misshapen chaos of well-seeming forms, feather of lead, bright smoke, cold fire, sick health", etc. (*R and J*, 1.181-4). Some passages in the Sonnets might owe a debt to Petrarch at least as much as to the other Platonist tradition to which I refer. (see William Melczer, *Neo-Platonism and Petrarchism, familiar or strange bed-fellows*, 1975). But Romeo's list

---

[8] Oswald Croll, transl. H. Pinnell, London 1657, p.214.
[9] Hegel was indebted to Boehme. See C. Taylor, *Hegel*, p520.
[10] In the Foreword to *Zur Farbenlehre*.

is ironically presented, and Petrarchism did not have the far-reaching philosophical and mystical implications that the *Symposium* and its successors have.

The *Symposium* mattered also to the Italian humanist Baldassare Castiglione, whose *Il Cortegiano* was translated as *The Courtier*, and was well known in Shakespeare's day. The part of it that concerns us is the conversation between Florentine ladies and gentlemen, debating 'whether women be not as meete for heavenly love as men'[11] meaning the heavenly love that Diotima speaks of. (Where Plato described a progression from the love of one man to the love of many, Castiglione writes 'And thus shall he beholde no more the particular beautie of one woman, but an universall, that decketh out all bodies'.)[12] There are some doubts among the company whether women can be altogether trusted not to misuse any licence granted, but despite this the argument continues, that kissing may be not merely sensual but a bond between souls. A man and a woman can 'power them selves by turne the one into the other bodie, and bee so mingled together, that each of them has two soules'. Once again 'Platonic love' is seen not as shunning erotic expression but as 'bringing forth' upon the beautiful in body as well as in soul. And besides, the exclusive privilege of men in attaining the vision of love is extended to women also. This affords Shakespeare a wider range than would be available if he had only encountered the *Symposium*.

The intermingling of tradition, Plato, neo-Platonism, alchemy, stretches still further when we find authors speaking of Christian parallels. For every base metal contained a kernel or seed of gold, surrounded by 'dross', and to remove this dross was to allow the gold itself to shine forth in splendour. For the Christian, this could be interpreted as freeing the soul from sin and allowing Christ to transmute and take over the reborn soul. Some alchemists spoke also of a blackening – probably observed when mercury was heated – known as the stage of 'nigredo', or death to the self. George Herbert (1593-1633) interpreted it in this way in 'The Elixir' (this being another name for the Stone):

All may of thee partake:
Nothing can be so mean,
Which with his tincture (for thy sake)
Will not grow bright and clean ...

---

[11] Castiglione, *The Courtier*, ed. J. Whitfield, p.324 (end of Book 4).
[12] *op.cit.* p.318.

This is the famous stone
That turneth all to gold:
For that which God doth touch and own
Cannot for lesse be told.[13]

Shakespeare, seldom making any explicit reference to Christ, was aware of the human parallel between the transmuting power of the Stone and the ability to influence other men and women. When Cleopatra praises Mark Antony, she compares a messenger from him with Antony himself, and concedes that the messenger has been a little changed:

How much unlike art thou Mark Antony
Yet, coming from him that *great med'cine* hath
With *his tinct gilded* thee.
(*A. and C.* 1.5.35-7)

Antony, like the medicine of the Elixir, has gone some way to turning the man into gold, gilding him. Similarly, Casca speaks of Brutus with admiration:

O, he sits high in all the people's hearts;
And that which would appear offence in us,
His countenance, like richest alchemy.
Will change to virtue and to worthiness.
(*J.C.* 1.3.150-160)

It seems that Shakespeare saw his lover, if only momentarily, as Cleopatra saw Antony in the passage I just quoted. That is the conclusion I draw from Sonnet 33 and 34, taking the two together. In the first he speaks as though he were 'turned to gold', by a sun which seems a parallel with his lover. In the second he fuses the identity of the lover with the sun. In other Sonnets, as I shall show, he himself is indistinguishable from either.

---

[13] For examples of Christ-symbolism in alchemy see C.G. Jung, *Die Erlösungsvorstellungen in der Alchemie*, Zurich 1947, pp.84-104. Also Jung, *Psychologie und Alchemie*, Zurich 1944. The mystical poet Henry Vaughan and his twin Thomas were strongly influenced by alchemical ideas. Milton's thoughtful man, 'Il Penseroso', studies 'thrice-great Hermes', Hermes Trismegistus, the legendary father of alchemy, after whom Tristram Shandy's father desired that his son should be named. Strindberg made alchemical experiments. Yeats wrote 'Rosa Alchemica'. Joyce referred to himself in *Finnegans Wake* as 'the first till last alshemist'.

Full many a glorious morning have I seene,
Flatter the mountaine tops with soveraine eie,
Kissing with golden face the meddowes greene;
Guilding pale streames with heavenly alcumy:
Anon permit the basest cloudes to ride,
With ougly rack on his celestiall face,
And from the for-lorne world his visage hide
Stealing unseene to west with this disgrace:
Even so my Sunne one early morne did shine,
With all triumphant splendor on my brow,
But out alack, he was but one houre mine,
The region cloude hath mask'd him from me now.
　　Yet him for this my love no whit disdaineth,
　　Suns of the world may staine, when heavens sun staineth.
(Sonnet 33)

In the first quatrain the sun is seen like a King – Louis XIV, 'le roi soleil' comes to mind – who shines on the mountain-tops as the King might shine on his courtiers, flattering them by illuminating their uncouth shapes; the sun goes on to kiss, and make the meadows look like gold, and 'gilding' streams too, with what is called 'heavenly', that is, not money-grubbing alchemy.

This is a poetic image, not an account of a real alchemical procedure. The natural scene is evoked by the alchemical parallels, but the next quatrain speaks of a more human effect. 'My Sunne' is of course the poet's lover, but he still acts like the sun in heaven coming with 'all triumphant splendour' on the poet's brow. We may also see him as transforming the poet, even if only for an hour, gilding him as the sun gilded the meadows and the stream. As readers, we now have to ask whether this is meant as mere ornament, hyperbole as flattery, sincere admiration, or to some degree a way of putting in poetry the experience of a great moment in the poet's life. 'All triumphant splendour', is apt for some transcending realisation more than for some mortal lover. 'Triumphant' in particular is suited to some being that by its or his great power is truly able to triumph. We should remember too what Touchstone says to Audrey, that 'the truest poetry is the most feigning' while still taking in the full power of poetry that acknowledges itself to be feigning.

Mystics often speak of the sun to convey, poetically rather than realistically, the nature of their vision. Jacob Boehme legendarily fell into a trance while gazing at a reflection of the sun in a polished metal plate. Evelyn Underhill[14] quotes many examples where for the mystics 'a new sun arises above the horizon and transfigures' their twilit world. W.H.

---

[14] Underhill, p.28.

Auden[15] believed indeed that 'the primary experience, complicated as it became later – out of which the Sonnets to the friend spring was a mystical one'. It may be that Sonnet 33 was in fact the origin of all the rest, although many of these are about love in its usual human sense.

The question is complicated by the fact that the poet's lover and the sun are in the next Sonnet inextricably identified with one another.

> Why didst thou promise such a beautious day,
> And make me travaile forth without my cloake,
> To let bace cloudes ore-take me in my way,
> Hiding thy brav'ry in their rotten smoke.
> Tis not enough that through the cloude thou breake,
> To dry the raine on my storme-beaten face,
> For no man well of such a salve can speake,
> That heales the wound, and cures not the disgrace:
> Nor can thy shame give phisicke to my griefe,
> Though thou repent, yet I have still the losse,
> Th'offenders sorrow lends but weake reliefe
> To him that beares the strong offenses losse.
> > Ah but those teares are pearle which thy love sheeds,
> > And they are ritch, and ransome all ill deeds.
>
> (Sonnet 34)

The Sonnet begins prosaically with a complaint. 'Thou' – that is, the poet's lover – has wrongly forecast a fair day, so that the poet went out without his cloak. But the 'bravry', the colourfulness of the man's dress or of his character is hidden by clouds, just as the sun was in the previous Sonnet, hiding him, and this is the man's fault: he has 'let' the clouds do this. But the charge is unfair: nobody can make the weather behave in one way or another.

In the second quatrain the man actually is the sun. It is no use breaking through the clouds to dry the poet's face, since this merely heals the wound, without curing the disgrace. The confusion of the man with the sun grows on as we read. What wound has the sun caused, what disgrace? Does the poet mean some rejection of love, symbolised by clouds masking that hurt? Has the lover suddenly taken the place of the sun? The sun can't 'repent' or feel 'sorrow' – unlikely consequences of having made a wrong weather forecast – Nor can the sun shed tears, as the final couplet says he does – it is surely the lover who sheds them, showing his love for the poet. Yet the tears may be rain, and the poet may be deceived in seeing them as signs of repentance.

---

[15] Auden, p.1726.

Going back to Sonnet 33, here is the same ambiguity. The sun that
shines on the poet's brow may be the sun, his human lover, or it may be
akin to the Philosophers' Stone, with its power to transmute. 'Suns of the
world may staine, when heavens sun staineth' (33.14). Both suns are the
same sun, as the poet sees them.

The ambiguity in both these Sonnets is found very often, throughout
the whole collection. Remaining within the field of alchemy, let us look
now at Sonnet 20.

A Womans face with natures owne hand painted,
Haste thou the Master Mistris of my passion,
A womans gentle hart but not acquainted
With shifting change as is false womens fashion,
An eye more bright then theirs, lesse false in rowling:
Gilding the object whereupon it gazeth,
A man in hew all *Hews* in his controwling,
Which steales mens eyes and womens soules amaseth.
And for a woman wert thou first created,
Till nature as she wrought thee fell a dotinge,
And by addition me of thee defeated,
By adding one thing to my purpose nothing.
    But since she prickt thee out for womens pleasure,
    Mine be thy love and thy loves use their treasure.
(Sonnet 20)

The first two lines are about a man whose appearance is as much
feminine as masculine. It has often been noticed that this suits the Earl of
Southampton, thought to have been the lover to whom the Sonnets are
addressed in the Dedication, the mysterious Mr W.H., their 'onlie
begetter'. 'Master Mistris' is less easily understood as meaning the Earl,
or any other lover: we do not call a male lover a 'master', nor does
'mistress' seem appropriate in terms of ordinary parlance, however
feminine the man's looks. The next couplet provides a hint: the lover's
eye, which for Elizabethans would illuminate the objects it sees, as by a
ray, and not by a light reflected from the object, as in the modern view,
gilds what it gazes on. Like the sun in Sonnet 33, it turns what it gazes at
into something resembling gold, perhaps, one may say, imparting its
quality to it as Antony and Brutus impart their own qualities.

'A man in hew all *Hews* in his controwling' is also open to more than
one interpretation. 'Hews' can mean 'hues', or 'shapes', objects that are
hewn. It can mean 'form, shape, figure'. By Oscar Wilde, it was taken,
humorously, to mean 'Hughes', a supposed boy-actor with whom
Shakespeare was in love. There may very well have been such a love for
one of the boys who played women's parts, and who might appear very

feminine when made up and dressed as a woman. This gives rise to the thought that 'controlling all figures', all characters, may have been the very power Shakespeare saw himself as possessing.   There will be more indications of this kind, that Shakespeare draws himself as 'the poet' identical with the lover. But the line is too difficult to interpret with any great sense of conviction, or do more than hint at these later indications.

On the other hand, the beginning of the third quatrain brings certainty. 'And for a woman wert thou first created' means both 'you were created at first to be woman' – your body was that of a woman – and 'you were created, like Adam ('first') to be a man for a woman, to satisfy a woman', with a hint that Eve is meant. The third quatrain then pursues the sense that the body is a woman's, but in order to say how Nature, feminine, was so in love with that body that in order to satisfy herself she added 'one thing to my purpose nothing'; she 'prickt ... out' the female body, selected it (as Brutus's conspirators prick out their victims) and provided a prick – the word was not thought vulgar as it is today – for the pleasure of women.[16]

The hermaphrodite figure was often used in alchemy as a symbol of perfection, the fusion of two opposites, even though these might also be called Sulphur and Mercury. (It is also known everywhere, from Leonardo's St John to the Hermaphrodite in the Borghese Gallery in Rome, to Polynesian sculptures. Michelangelo, writing love-sonnets both to a man and a woman, sometimes addressed the woman as 'Signor'. The dual figure is the subject of a poem by Ovid, and of one by John Barnfield in Shakespeare's day. Mignon in Goethe's *Wilhelm Meister* continues the tradition.

Sonnet 20 is more witty than beautiful as Sonnet 33 is. It is, however, another instance, like 34, of the mingling of reality with symbolism. The first three lines can be read as meaning a man, as can the final couplet. In between, the hermaphrodite is intelligible only in symbolic terms. But as the sun is symbolic in 34, while the beginning and ending are understandable in terms of a man, so in 20 we are continually invited to see both at once, the symbol and the real figure. The Master Mistress is a Philosophers' Stone, so far as gilding goes, also a man of feminine appearance, and a being of dual sex, all three mingling.[17]

The hermaphrodite is suggested again in Sonnet 53:

---

[16] 'To my purpose nothing' implies the poet had no interest in any homoerotic pleasure. However, Hamlet taunts Ophelia with the idea that 'nothing' can mean what lies 'between a maid's legs' *(Hamlet* 3.2.126). This leaves the question of the poet's sexual inclination entirely unanswered. The poet is in any case not identical with Shakespeare.

[17] See Marie Delcourt, *Hermaphrodite.*

Describe *Adonis* and the counterfet [portrait],
Is poorely imitated after you,
On *Hellens* cheeke all art of beautie set,
And you in Grecian tires [clothes] are painted new.

The acme of male and female beauty is present in the lover, but this is more than saying, as it might be said of the Earl of Southampton, that there is some feminine quality in his masculine appearance. Such a combination is conceivable only in terms of some ideal being, such as the one suggested in the opening lines of the same Sonnet:

What is your substance, whereof are you made,
That millions of strange shaddowes on you tend?
Since every one hath, every one, one shade,
And you but one can every shaddow lend:
(53.1-4)

'Substance' in the Platonic sense is the essential nature underlying phenomena. The poet asks what the lover's substance may be, since millions of strange shadows tend on him, as those phenomena 'tend' on the substance. The answer must be the centre to which the lover is so often compared, and is even identified: the sun. It can surely be said of a mere man that he is so attended, but the sun *is* 'but one' and yet can make shadows all around itself. (Might Shakespeare not also have seen himself in this passage, feeling amazed at his prolific imagination, capable of creating so many characters out of the thousands, if not millions, of others swarming in his mind? This is another point at which one begins to see him in this way, 'controwling' all hues (20.7) and as identifying himself with his lover.)

Mystical visions usually require a period of fasting or denial of self, yet Shakespeare does not speak of any in close connection wit the Sonnets where a vision is involved. But the Sonnets do not form a coherent presentation. Shakespeare is not a philosopher with a system to be expanded, or a religious giving a close account of his progress. Sonnets with affinity to one another may be widely separated, as 146 is separated from 33, although it provides just such an instance of self-disdain as usually precedes a vision. Why, the poet asks his soul, does she spend so much time on wearing costly garments, when worms will eat up all she has and is. Is she aware of the shortness of her life?

Buy tearmes divine in selling hours of drosse:
Within be fed, without be rich no more,

So shalt thou feed on death, that feeds on men,
And death once dead, there's no more dying then.
(146.11-14)

('Death, thou shalt die' (Holy Sonnets XX) – here and in several other
Sonnets, as we shall see, there is a close resemblance to Donne.) But what
has this to do with love? A great deal, if we think of the long tradition in
which lovers are said to be identical with one another. I am thine, you are
mine, you are enclosed in my bosom, and the key is lost, so it must always
be', reads a twelfth century German poem whose sense is often repeated,
as it is in Sidney's 'My true love hath my hart, and I have his'. It merely
means that the lovers are for ever closely bound to one another, without
'impediment' (116.2) in their marriage, the one always aligning with the
other despite differences. Shakespeare takes the idea more literally. Just
as in the dual sex of the lover in Sonnet 20, he makes the lover and the
poet literally one, and does so in language that has itself two meanings. In
Sonnet 24 the confusion of identities is almost impossible to comprehend.
(The beauty of the lover is in the poet's heart, but to see it one must look
through the lover's eyes, which are windows to the poet's breast, even
though they are windows to the poet's 'shop'.) A little later, the poet
speaks as though his lover enclosed not only himself but all his friends:

Their images I lovd, I view in thee,
And thou (all they) hast all the all of me.
(31.13-14)

as though all were completely one. And yet, soon after, he contradicts
himself

Let me confesse, that we two must be twaine,
Although our undevided loves are one.
(36.1-2)

And yet again, even as he confesses that the two must live divided (39.6)
he retracts, reflecting

… that thou teachest how to make one twaine,
By praising him here who doth hence remaine.
(39.13-14)

These two lines present opposite meanings all the way. 'Twaine' means
both 'divided in two' and 'a pair, two together'. Thus the lover's lesson is
at one and the same time that the poet and himself are separate, and that
they are united. The second of the lines is a play on the ambiguity of

'hence', which means 'not here', and 'therefore'. By praising the poet, who stays far off, the lover also makes him remain with him.

The contradictories are verbal. But then the whole ambiguous description of the lover is verbal too. The poet achieves thereby an atmosphere of uncertainty within certainty, a constant oscillation. (Once again Donne writes in the same vein, though really quite differently:

> Oh, to vex me, contraryes meet in me:
> Inconstancy unnaturally hath begott
> A constant habit ...
> (Holy Sonnet XIX)

For Donne the contradiction is painful: he praises God at one moment, and at another 'quakes with fear' of him as the Sonnets poet seems to do in Sonnet 90, welcoming the lover's hatred, and in 109, with its assurance that he can never lose his love. His 'best dayes' are nevertheless, those when he 'shakes with feare', but he is less wholly committed to contradictoriness than Shakespeare is.) Shakespeare, however, realises the 'contraryes' to which Donne refers, in more powerful language. For all the abundant love he speaks of, his lover can be like a monster. Donne may say he quakes, Shakespeare shows us what that means:

> Then hate me when thou wilt, if ever, now,
> Now while the world is bent my deeds to crosse,
> Joyne with the spight of fortune, make me bow,
> And doe not drop in for an after losse:
> Ah doe not, when my heart hath scapte this sorrow,
> Come in the rereward of a conquerd woe ...
> (90.1-6)

What love-poem ever spoke in such terms of total dereliction? The only parallel is surely the chapter in *Job*, where Job says of God

> He teareth me in his wrath, who hateth me: he gnasheth upon me with his teeth; mine enemy sharpeneth his eyes upon me ... God hath delivered me to the ungodly and turned me over into the hands of the wicked. I was at ease, but he hath broken me asunder: he hath also broken me by my neck, and shaken me to pieces, and set me up for his mark.
> (*Job* 16.9-12)

Sonnet 90 is the counterpart to the sonnets of pure love. It is written with full conviction.

How these paradoxes appear when transferred to the real world, if only the real world of theatre, we can see from Sonnet 40.

Take all my loves, my love, yea take them all.
What hast thou then more then thou hadst before?
(40.1-2)

(The lover is seen as Jesus might be seen by a nun about to take her vows of chastity. Great unselfishness is needed, but Jesus did on one occasion explicitly require it in anyone who really followed his teaching:

> If any man come to me, and hate not his father, and mother, and wife, and children, and brethren, and sisters, yea, and his own life also, he cannot be my disciple. (*Luke* 14.26)[18]

However, Jesus does not here draw these other loves into himself.)

In answer to the question, what the lover will have by the addition of the poet's love, that he did not have before, since 'All mine was thine', the poet continues

> Then if for my love, thou my love receivest,
> I cannot blame thee, for my love thou usest
> (40.4-5)

On this occasion the poet puns on 'my love' saying both that his love is not love at all ('my love' being vocative) and that it may be called true love ('thou mayest call my love true love'). It is already apparent that the lover has fallen in love with the poet's mistress. In giving the lover all his loves the poet means to include her. But this is no gift to a transcendent love that contains all the poet's love. The lover 'uses' the mistress, which in Sonnets parlance means he has sexual intercourse with her, and to say that this is acceptable because she is the poet's love sounds all too much like self-deception; in fact the poet continues in the remainder of the Sonnet to express his grief.

Elsewhere Shakespeare mocks the whole idea of such a willing sacrifice when the clown (Lavatch) argues:

> He that comforts my wife is the cherisher of my flesh and blood; he that cherishes my flesh and blood loves my flesh and blood; he that loves my flesh and blood is my friend; ergo he that kisses my wife is my friend. (*A.W.T.E.W.* 1.3.46-50)

In *The Two Gentlemen of Verona* there is a scene exactly reflecting the Sonnet, so far as yielding a mistress to another is concerned. Proteus and

---

[18] It is said that he meant not 'hate', but 'prefer rather than me', but the New Standard Revised Version retains 'hate'. It substitutes 'life itself' for 'his own life'.

Valentine are two close friends, who are both in love with Silvia. Proteus having expressed shame, after he has tried to rape Silvia, Valentine forgives him:

> And that my love may appear plain and free,
> All that was mine in Silvia I give thee.
> (*T.G.V.*5.482-3)

His motive may be pure, but takes no account of Silvia's feelings. Silvia does not say a word till the end of the play, and though an actress may show some displeasure on her behalf, Valentine's resignation must appear grossly unaware of not only Silvia's unwillingness, but masterful in its supposition that he can dispose of her at will.

In *The Merchant of Venice* Bassanio tells Antonio, who is likely to lose his life because of his generosity towards his friend, that he loves him beyond measure:

> Antonio, I am married to a wife
> Which is as dear to me as life itself;
> But life itself, my wife and all the world
> Are not with me esteemed above thy life.
> I would lose all, ay sacrifice them all
> Here to this devil [Shylock], to deliver you
> (*M.V.* 4.1.282-6)

Portia, still disguised as a man, comments

> Your wife would give you little thanks for that
> If she were by to hear you make that offer.
> (*M.V.* 4.1.287-8)

What appears in the Sonnet as generosity is rejected in the play.

Not all the contrasts are paradoxes. Some may be the experience of one moment compared with that of another. The poet comforts himself with the assurance that he cannot fail to be loved (25.13-14), but at once laments his unworthiness (26.14). He is unable to sleep for thoughts of his love, yet a moment of awareness restores him to complete assurance (29.13-14). Time will take his love away (64.12), but he hopes for a miracle, that 'in black inck my love may still shine bright' (65.14). These are the hopes and fears of any lover, ranged alongside one another rather than simultaneously present. But there are others, some of which have already been seen, that Samuel Johnson certainly would have included in his condemnation of puns as will-o'-the-wisp that led Shakespeare astray, even though puns were regarded as perfectly acceptable in Elizabethan and

Jacobean England. It is not simply a matter of using words with double meanings, as when Lady Macbeth speaks of implying guilt when she gilds the faces of Duncan's grooms with blood. Word-play in the Sonnets often involves meanings essential to the poet's purpose, in such a way that neither meaning is to be seen as invalidating or replacing the other. We have seen the play on 'twaine' in Sonnet 39. Similar is the thought in 40, where the poet asks what the lover has more than he had before, even when the poet has yielded to him all his loves. He will have

> No love, my love, that thou maist true love call
> (40.3)

The lover will receive no love worth calling love, and yet it will be the poet's love, and thus true in its own way, 'my love' serving as vocative and possessive, both equally.

Shielding his lover from blame, the poet declares himself the lover's defence:

> For to thy sensuall fault I bring in sence,
> Thy adverse party is thy Advocate.
> (35.9-10)

The spelling 'sence' suggests not only 'I bring (good) sense to bear (I see it as a fault)' but also 'incense': 'I reason about your behaviour but all the time I am wafting my adoration towards you'.

In praising the lover as the spring and harvest of the year, the poet suggests a kind of Eros when he adds:

> In all externall grace you have some part,
> But you like none, none you for constant heart
> (53.13-14)

Reading 'like' as an adjective, this gives: 'nobody compares with you for constancy'. Reading it as a verb, the opposite results: 'You do not favour anyone for being constant'. Both meanings suit Eros in that he inspires both flirting and long-lasting devotion.

> More important for the Sonnets as a whole are the lines
> Lascivious grace in whom all il wel showes,
> Kill me with spights yet we must not be foes
> (40.13-14)

'In whom all il wel showes' means both that the ill shows well, all too clearly, and that it is well. This is more than the kind of defence lovers make when they forgive, putting the ill to one side. Both are equally and simultaneously present: the ill shows all the time, while at the same time it is pronounced good. The opposites come together but are not fused so as to be seen as one; they remain in a dual relationship even as they are one. This is the way Shakespeare lives with his vision of universal love: it is never forsaken, never triumphant, but holds both sides in tension.

The search for such double meanings must have been deliberate. At times it could lead the poet completely astray, as in the lines

How have mine eies out of their Spheares bene fitted
In the distraction of this madding fever?
(119.7-8)

The poet intends to say that his passion is so great that it distorts his vision. 'Fitted', it is true, is not found anywhere else but in this one instance, and the O.E.D. respectfully interprets it as 'forced by fits or paroxysms out of (the usual place)'. It is the only instance quoted. However, the Quarto printing, clearly intended by Shakespeare, reads 'bene fitted'. Two lines later we have 'O benefit of ill'. The purpose is to say that the poet's eyes have been wrenched out of shape, and yet simultaneously he has benefited by this. Shakespeare might have said in his defence, if, with the self-assurance he shows in other Sonnets, he defended himself at all, that by setting himself free to commit such solecisms he could be free to write superbly at other times.

Much more ambitious, and difficult to comprehend, is Shakespeare's treatment of the final scene in *Romeo and Juliet*. The story as he found it was based on a theme highly popular in Renaissance Europe. In his adaptation it follows fairly closely the narrative poem by Arthur Brooke, *The Tragicall Historye of Romeo and Juliet*, printed in 1562 and reissued in 1587. In the poem, the deaths of the lovers are seen as rightful punishment for their sinful loves, a judgment that is unlikely to have appealed to Shakespeare. He differs also from other versions of the story, denying the lovers one last tragic meeting in the tomb. Instead, he introduces a scene based on a story in Ovid's *Metamorphoses*, the story of Pyramus and Thisbe. This is the same story as the one enacted in *A Midsummer Night's Dream* by Bottom the weaver and his actors, complete with Moonshine, the crack in the wall, and the lovers' mistakes: Thisbe is wounded by a lion and escapes. Pyramus finds the bloodstained cloak, supposes she has been killed, and kills himself. Thisbe returns, sees Pyramus's dead body, hugs it, and kills herself with the same sword. It is one of the most hilarious scenes in all the plays ever performed. In the tragedy, however, Romeo finds Juliet apparently dead, although in fact drugged unconscious, and kills himself; Juliet, awakening, tries to drink any of the poison left in Romeo's cup or on his lips, fails, and kills herself with his dagger. The same sequence of actions and motives is used for both the farce and the tragedy, though the speeches of the two lovers are distinguished by their great poetry. Both plays were written at about the same time.

Shakespeare could not have intended his theatre audiences to be aware of the parallels in two distinct plays. The parallels were certainly present in his own mind, but in what way he regarded them is still mysterious. He surely did not want to ridicule the tragedy by comparison with the farce, as he seems to have done in writing the scene in *Twelfth Night* where Malvolio wears yellow stockings and cross-garters, because he believes Olivia loves him and requires it. In the Sonnet, the poet offers his complete submission in the words 'Speake of my lamenesse, and I straight will halt' (89.3) but this does not seem fanciful unless we place it alongside Malvolio's devotion. In *Romeo and Juliet*, however, the intrusion of the Pyramus and Thisbe theme simply passes unrecognised. No audience is likely to think of the farcical version, and yet Shakespeare clearly held both farce and tragedy in mind. What might be a devastating comparison simply shows Shakespeare's own consciousness.

Another comparison of a similar kind concerns the apparent confession in Sonnet 33 that the poet has had an experience of a kind of vision expressed in terms of being touched by the Philosophers' Stone, which corresponds with the avowal of Sonnet 124 that his love is like the universal love described by Diotima. When Bottom the Weaver wakes up from the ecstatic embrace of Titania – named after a great god – he reflects on what he calls 'a most rare vision', which he also calls a dream 'past the wit of man to say what dream it was' (*A.M.N.D.* 4.1.200-219). Only a clown ('a patched fool') would try, he says, to say anything at all about what he thought he dreamed. 'The eye of man hath not heard, the ear of man hath not seen, man's hand is not able to taste, nor his tongue to conceive, nor his heart to report what my dream was'. He is of course misquoting St Paul: 'the wisdom of God is a mystery, even the hidden wisdom, which God ordained before the world unto our glory' (I *Cor.* 2.7). 'Eye hath not seen, nor ear heard, neither have entered into the heart of man, the things which God hath prepared for them that love him' (I *Cor.* 2.9). Bottom garbles this famous passage, transposing the verb to inappropriate senses. But it is significant, given Shakespeare's frequent identification of opposites, that Bottom thinks of St Paul at all. When he adds, comically enough, that his dream 'shall be called "Bottom's Dream", because it hath no bottom', he may recall Rosalind's words to Celia: 'O coz, coz, coz, my pretty little coz, that thou didst know how many fathoms deep I am in love! But it cannot be sounded. My affection hath an unknown bottom, like the Bay of Portugal'. To this Celia replies 'Or, rather, bottomless, that as fast as you pour affection in, it runs out' (*A.Y.L.I.* 4.1.2-4-8). Either way, the bottomless dream of Bottom is the dream of love, as the words of St Paul, even when garbled, would lead one to expect.

What impelled Shakespeare to make such a strange combination is beyond guessing. He could have been inspired by an overwhelming modesty, unwilling to say without contradiction or parallel that the vision of Sonnet 33 was really his. He may have scorned the same vision, mocking it by attributing something of the same kind to such a man as Bottom. He may have simply created an opposition in accordance with the philosophy of alchemy and Renaissance neo-Platonism – though that sounds the least likely explanation. Going to such lengths as he does to involve Bottom in his own experience looks more serious. The fact remains that this dream is one of many other opposites that he tries to bring into one. His mind would seem to be always straddling them both, never committed to one or the other and yet totally committed to both: he loves totally and mocks or denies totally.

CHAPTER TWO

THE YOUNG MAN AND THE MISTRESS

The young man is so vividly present in Sonnet after Sonnet, that readers are convinced he must have been a real person. No certainty has ever been achieved. The Mr W.H. who is described in the Dedication as 'the onlie begetter' may have been William Herbert, Earl of Pembroke, but so little is said in detail that would confirm this or any of the other candidates as Shakespeare's lover. It sometimes feels as though what Cleopatra says of Antony provides a clue, not pointing to any particular man, but to the way in which Shakespeare saw him in his imagination. When the Queen demands of Dolabella to know whether the Romans think what she says of Antony is true or false. She tells him of a dream in which

His face was as the heav'ns, and therein stuck
A sun and moon, which kept their course and lighted
This little 'O', the earth.
His legs bestrid the ocean, his reared arm
Crested the world ... In his livery [guardianship]
Walked crowns and crownets: realms and islands were
As plates [silver coins] dropped from his pocket
(*A. and C.* 5.2.79-92)

(Sun and moon together are a common symbol of perfection in alchemy.) Dolabella attempts to interrupt, but she asks:

Think you there was or might be such a man
As this I dreamt of?

and when he politely expresses his disbelief she bursts into passionate affirmation:

You lie, up to the hearing of the gods.
(*A. and C.* 5.2.93-95)

She must know perfectly well that she is asking the impossible, or she would not ask Dolabella. But her retort is not ironic. She affirms her extravagance with equal vehemence

> But if there be nor ever were one such,
> It's past the size of dreaming;

She does not say 'it would be', but 'it is', reiterating even as she allows for doubt.

>   nature wants stuff
> To vie strange forms with fancy, yet t'imagine
> An Antony were nature's piece 'gainst fancy,
> Condemning shadows quite
> (*A. and C.* 5.2.95-99)

Nature lacks the material to compete with what can be imagined, but if Nature *could* imagine it would be a triumph over imagination, more real than any dream-like shadows. The proof that what she has dreamed is a reality depends upon Nature being able to equal her in imagination. Yet her absolute certainty, for a moment, that her dream of Antony is no illusion is unmistakable.

It may be that Shakespeare regarded his impossible praises and comparisons in the same way, defying reason and yet realising that reason could not be disregarded: 'it's past the size of dreaming'.

There was much talk in his day of the Real Presence, prolonging the debate of centuries over whether the 'substance' of the bread and wine in the Eucharist was changed by consecration into the body and blood of Christ, while the 'accidents' remained unchanged. (The love spoken of in Sonnet 124 was 'buylded far from accident', although the context there was Platonic.) Luther held that the bread and wine co-existed with the body and the blood, others maintained there was a change in the elements, that they were symbols, while others insisted on the real presence, substance and accidents in one, rather as Cleopatra insisted that her dream was a reality, without diminution. The earlier controversy over the divine and the human natures of Christ, resolved in the affirmation that he was 'very man and very god', was of a similar kind. Subconsciously or not, Shakespeare could have thought in this connection that an ideal figure could conceivably be fully present in reality. There would have been the same difficulties as in the Christian's dogma, since the young man can be very human, as when he robs the poet of his mistress, just as the physical nature of Christ's body gave rise to doubts whether he could also be divine.

I do not argue that the young man is best regarded as a 'Christ-figure'. There are, however, several occasions in the Sonnets when a Christian parallel is invoked. The poet says he makes no claim to be saying anything new about his love,

> but yet like prayers divine,
> I must each day say ore the very same,
> Counting no old thing old, thou mine, I thine,
> Even as when first I hallowed thy fair name.
> (108.5-8)

In the Lord's Prayer, it is the name of God the Father that is to be hallowed, made holy. Borrowing the word, the poet gains a great weight of traditional meaning, indeed making 'antiquitie for aye his page'. This is exactly the kind of praise Cleopatra gives to Antony.

Similarly, the poet writes

> 'Gainst death and all oblivious enmity
> Shall you pace forth.
> (55.9-10)

There are many mentions in both Old and New Testaments of death being conquered, as in *2 Timothy* 1.10: 'our Saviour Jesus Christ, who hath abolished death', and in *1 Corinthians* 15.26, 'The last enemy that shall be destroyed is death'. That a real man such as the Sonnets lover should 'pace forth' so resolutely is hard to imagine. But Shakespeare does imagine it, and insists on the reader's acceptance, despite all such incredulity as a Dolabella might display.

Perhaps we can see a similar allusion in Sonnet 117, when the poet confesses he has

> scanted all
> Wherein I should your great deserts repay
> … And given to time your owne deare purchasd right …
> (117.1-2 and 6)

Nothing is said to show what great deserts might be meant, but the dear purchased right sounds rather like St Paul when he says 'Ye are bought [by Christ] with a price; (*1 Cor* 6.20) and the reference in *Acts* 20.28 to 'the church of God, which he hath purchased with his own blood'. The great deserts must then surely allude to Christ's merits by which mankind was saved. The image of the young man becomes even greater with these allusions, although it may have had no corresponding reality of its own.

The eyes that 'taught the dumbe on high to sing' (78.5) recall the prediction in *Isaiah* 35.6, 'Then shall the lame man leap as an hart, and the tongue of the dumb sing'. This is about some future time when a Jewish Messiah will come down to begin a reign of peace. Without specifically alluding to Christ, Sonnet 106 portrays many generations celebrated by poets, of 'Ladies dead and lovely Knights', all drawn without awareness of the beauty of the young man.

> So all their praises are but prophesies
> Of this our time, all you prefiguring.
> (106.9-10)

Although the progression is of beauty succeeding beauty, a parallel is the Christian belief, plentifully illustrated in the Sistine Chapel, that pagan poets, Virgin and the Sibyls and the prophets all foretold the coming of Christ. Vasari, indeed, had spoken analogously of Michelangelo as an artist 'acclaimed as divine', who had been sent by heaven to reveal the true nature of art, hitherto only poorly understood by his predecessors. Shakespeare is very likely to have heard this praise of an artist as though he were a saviour.

Completely unserious is Sonnet 105 claiming that the poet is not idolatrous in praising his lover, because he is fair, kind and true, 'three theams in one', alluding to the Holy Trinity, but in entirely unreligious terms.

Yet with all this, the young man is clearly identified with Eros in Sonnet 126, where he is 'my lovely Boy [boy Cupid]' whose lovers wither even as he himself grows, and who has 'by wayning growne'. There are many erotic passages in the Sonnets, and though it is surprising to find Eros mentioned as though there were nothing dividing him from Christ, in Renaissance times it was often thought that pagan deities and heroes either foreshadowed or were equivalents of figures in Christian and Jewish tradition. Solon and Moses the lawgivers, the chaste Diana and the Virgin Mary, the strong men Hercules and Samson were all seen in this light. Eros himself was described in the *Symposium* in terms strangely resembling one description of Christ in his own words:

> nor is he delicate and lovely, as most of us believe, but harsh and arid, barefoot and homeless, sleeping on naked earth, in doorways, or in the very streets beneath the stars of heaven, and always partaking of his mother's poverty. (*Symposium* 203)

How this came to be written several centuries before Christ is a mystery. But the similarity can't be doubted:

> The foxes have holes, and the birds of the air have nests; but the Son of
> Man hath not where to lay his head. (*Matthew* 8.20)

Shakespeare may well have noticed this when he read the *Symposium*.

Yet more difficult to understand are several passages in the Sonnets
when the poet speaks of himself and his lover as one. He excuses his self-
love on the grounds that

> 'Tis thee (my selfe) that for my self I praise.
> (62.13)

and, with a play on his own name that he exploits to the full in two of the
Sonnets about the Mistress:

> O therefore love be of thy selfe so wary,
> As I not for my selfe but for thee will.
> (22.10-11)

'For thee will' means both 'as I will be wary for you' and 'I, Will, am for
thee, am Will for thee'. The same play on his name is in

> So true a foole is love, that in your Will,
> (Though you do any thing) he thinkes no ill.
> (57.13-14)

This time the Quarto prints a capital 'W', making more clearly visible the
sense that Will submits willingly to love, and that he is love's will.

These are not merely cold-hearted puns. In other places the poet
speaks with great tenderness, when he finds his love 'within the gentle
closure of my brest' (48.11), and with passion in

> For nothing this wide Universe I call,
> Save thou my Rose, in it thou art my all.
> (109.13-14)

Even so, the lover's infidelities are strongly in the poet's mind. He
proffers excuses: roses have thorns, fountains make mud (35.2), and then
blames himself for doing so:

> All men make faults, and even I in this,
> Authorizing thy trespass with compare,
> My selfe corrupting salving thy amisse.
> (35.5-7)

He knows perfectly well that the excuses are lame, but makes them all the
same. It is part of the defence he makes when he says that in his lover 'all
il wel showes' (40.13) – the ill shows up clearly and yet shows as though it
were well.

In an extreme form, the poet writes here as though thinking of Christ's
injunction to

> Love your enemies, bless them that curse you, do good to them that hate
> you, and pray for them which despitefully use you, and persecute you.
> (*Matthew* 5.44)

Though the lover does not curse the poet, or persecute him, his spirit is the
same, as he continually puts himself last. In one way he goes further than
Jesus's advice to make peace with one's accuser on the way to court, rather
than in the trial itself (*Matthew* 5.25). The poet is in the court, his lover's
advocate, putting the case against himself (35.10). There is nothing like
this in Plato.   Shakespeare inherited the submissiveness from long-
standing, partly Christian tradition.

As to the restriction of the lover to the self of the poet, we may
understand that this is meant in the sense that all the poet ever imagines is
still a creation of his own, not a realisation of a being 'out there'.

The role of the mistress is in many ways like that of the lover. She is
denounced for her infidelity more strongly than he is, and the poet is
erotically attracted to her as he never is to the man, but his love is tested by
her just as it is by the man. For 'all il wel showes' we have 'all my best
doth worship thy defect' (149.11) and 'Whence hast thou this becomming
of things il' (150.5). But the paradox existed in Shakespeare's mind
perhaps even before he began to write either plays or Sonnets.

The mistress is not a 'Dark Lady'. The euphemism ignores the fact that
she is never called 'dark', but always 'black', and is not particularly
ladylike. The earliest mention of such blackness as hers comes in *Love's
Labour's Lost* when the King of Navarre and his courtiers unaccountably
turn against Berowne's Rosaline, calling her black, over and over again.
They imply she is ugly, although the King goes further when he says
'Black is the badge of hell, the hue of dungeons' (*L.L.L.* 4.3.251),
suggesting vaguely some evil quality. Berowne, however, replies 'No face
is fair that is not full so black' (*L.L.L.* 4.3.250), thus announcing the theme
of several Sonnets. In another early play, the black man Aaron sees a
nurse trying to hide his black child from sight, because it is 'as loathsome
as a toad', 'a devil', and protests:

Is black so base a hue?
Sweet blowze, you are a beauteous blossom, sure.
(*T.A.* 4.2.71-2)

The two passages together show Shakespeare toying with the idea, at this very early stage, that there is a paradox in blackness that may extend not only to beauty but to morality. He could have picked up the idea from hearing about paradox in the philosophy of Giordano Bruno when he came to England in 1583. He may also have been struck by the verse in *The Song of Solomon* where the beloved woman says she is 'black but comely', though there is no moral implication in that (*S. of S.* 1.5) But there is no satisfying explanation why the idea should have taken such root.

It is puzzling too, that in the Sonnets many mentions of 'black' carry no paradoxical meaning at all, as though the word itself were the attraction. Only about half of Sonnets 127-154, where the mistress is mostly mentioned, are about moral blackness. Some are trivial, if sometimes in an agreeable way: the mistress mourns in her black eyes the women who adorn themselves with cosmetics; her eyes mourn the pain she causes the poet by disdaining him. In reply he tells her punningly that her morning eyes become her and that she should go on mourning for him so that he may say 'beauty herselfe is blacke' (132.13). The pretty compliment, contrasting with so much else in the Sonnets, also contrasts with Donne, who, almost as though he had Shakespeare's Sonnets in mind, urges his black soul to make itself 'with holy mourning blacke', repenting (*Holy Sonnet* IV). Other Sonnets in this group are not concerned with blackness at all: the poet envies the harpsichord keys that are kissed by his mistress's fingers; he compares her to a housewife chasing a chicken; he thinks his mistress hates him, till 'I hate, from hate away she threw' (145.13) with an allusion to Anne Hathaway that suggests a very early date of composition; the mistress kills him with disdain, but they must not be foes: let her at least pretend to love him. Of quite a different kind is the ferocious denunciation of lust: 'savage, extreame, rude, cruell, not to trust' (129.4) and the advice by the poet to himself to renounce all care for the body (146.13-14).

The 'two loves I have of comfort and despaire' (144.1), the one a handsome man, the other a 'woman colloured il', have often been taken inappropriately to refer to the man and the woman in the rest of the Sonnets, but the last six lines makes this unlikely: the poet imagines the one may have 'turn'd finde', and he suspects one 'angel' is already in bed with the other. This cynicism allows no such distinction as the first lines may suggest. The Sonnet has no coherence with the rest, and may have been sparked off by having seen Marlowe's Faustus between his good and his bad angel.

There is at first no clear portrayal of the mistress as anything but admirable even in her so-called 'blackness'. In Sonnet 131, however, the poet speaks of the mistress as 'tirranous' by her very nature, 'so as thou art', and yet not cruel as other women who torment by their beauty. He acknowledges that others say she has no beauty that could make a man groan, but here again he adds

> Thy blacke is fairest in my judgments place.
> (131.12)

This is not quite unqualified praise. 'In my judgment' would be enough to confirm the poet's steadfast view, but adding 'in my judgments place' hints at 'in place of my judgment': the poet judges this to be so, but veers a little towards an opposite view. However, the equation of 'black' and 'fairest' is present, even though said of a mistress who tyrannizes. The poet maintains the paradox even as he ambiguously disavows his own capacity to judge aright.

His judgment is faulty in the line 'In nothing art thou blacke save in thy deeds' (151.13), which denies what it affirms to no effect. It may be, however, that the mistress is pure in intention, and only appears otherwise in her actions, or that the sheer fact of her ability to make him groan, despite her lack of good looks, is her saving grace. This echoes what is said of the man, whom people continually misjudge. They praise him to the skies, but confound themselves

> By seeing farther than the eye hath showne
> They looke into the beauty of thy mind.
> And that in guesse they measure by thy deeds
> (69.8-10)

and churlishly accuse him of wrongdoing, when he is really innocent. But this reverses the situation: the woman is only black in her deeds, while her mind is pure; the man's bad deeds lead people to suppose his deeds are a key to his mind. The oscillation leaves the reader uncertain how to interpret. Indeed the deeds and the motives are so indefinite, constant reassertions that all is good and well begin to look too mechanical.

This defence of the mistress becomes increasingly difficult to maintain. It is so often made, one suspects, because it allows the poet to go on believing his love is universal, able to meet difficulties by asserting that they don't exist. The poet speaks of 'the very refuse of thy deeds' (150.6) which exceeds 'all best', and attempts to justify this with the thought that someone has taught her how to make him love her more the more he sees reason to hate her:

Oh though I love what others doe abhor,
With others thou shouldst not abhor my state.
If thy unworthinesse raisd love in me,
More worthy I to be belov'd of thee
(150.11-14)

But what is it they abhor? If 'raised' means sexually aroused, the poet is affirming here that this fact of his human nature and its sexuality counts for more than any fault of the mistress's character, as indeed he does say in the next Sonnet, where he asks her not to spell out his own faults (she does not) lest this makes her all the readier to yield to his wooing ('Least guilty of my faults thy sweet selfe prove' (151.4)

For thou betraying me, I doe betray
My nobler part to my grose bodies treason,
My soule doth tell my body that he may,
Triumph in love, flesh staies no farther reason,
But rising at thy name doth point out thee.

It is as though his erect phallus had a will of its own, a capacity to override his 'nobler part', and to be accepted in that. In his transports he must have felt so: the attraction of sexual fulfilment *is* overwhelming, once it is fully admitted. But the poet maintains his defence by the dubious means of saying his conscience is satisfied:

Love is too young to know what conscience is,
Yet who knowes not conscience is borne of love
151.1-2)

and ending
No want of conscience hold it that I call,
Her love, for whose deare love I rise and fall
(151.13-14)

Two meanings of 'conscience' are involved here, both 'guardian of morality' and 'to be privy with another in a matter' (*O.E.D.*), that is, 'conscire', to know with, and 'to know right and wrong'. This makes the poet's defence inadequate on any serious level. The contradictions have too little definiteness to allow their combinations to be meaningful.

The underlying thought in those defences of erotic values may well be akin to Lear's outrage at the beadle who flogs the prostitute, when all the while the man lusts after her himself. As Kenneth Muir points out, this in

turn owes something to Montaigne's revolutionary treatment of sex.[21] But
better use of this liberal treatment of erotic attraction is found in other
Sonnets.[22]

Incidentally, the Sonnets addressed to the man never deny his beauty,
or suggest any sexual relationship with him. There are, however, several
similarities between him and the mistress. He is blamed and then excused
for his inconstancy, and there are times when his reputation is blackened,
even as it is paradoxically defended (40.13). More than this, the poet does
not distinguish between himself and the man: 'Tis thee (my selfe) that for
my self I praise' (62.13). So there is an ambiguity when the poet
complains that he and his lover are rivals in love, both of them loving the
same woman: 'Both finde each other, and I lose both twaine' (47.11), and
yet 'Me from my selfe thy cruell eye hath taken' (133.5). But yet again 'I
my selfe am morgag'd to thy [the mistress's] will' (134.2) which may be
compared with 'not for my selfe but for thee [the man] will' (22.10) and
with 'So will I pray that thou [the mistress] maist have thy *Will*' (143.13
'Will' italicized in the Quarto). Again, the man is said to have 'all the all
of me' (31.14) while the poet is 'pent in thee [the mistress]' and is
'perforce … thine and all that is in me' (133.14). Since in one sense the
man contains both sexes (20 and 53) addressing the one may often be to
address the other. In all these instances the mind is dazzled by the
continual dual reference. Yet while there are in the 'Mistress' Sonnets no
such allusions to Christ as are made in regard to the man, there is
especially in Sonnets 135 and 136 a combination of both sexes in the word
'will' that results in an extraordinary parallel to the Sonnet in which a
mystical vision is spoken of (33.9-10) and Diotima's description of a
related ecstasy (124.5-12). If the poet can sustain his paradoxical view of
his lover's beauty, he can maintain that vision unharmed.

The moment of revelation in Sonnet 33 and the other passages
concerning the possibility of a supreme revelation have no mention of any
erotic union. Yet in mystical writings some such union is quite often
involved, as in St Teresa of Avila's ecstasy, and when Diotima herself
mysteriously defines love as 'to bring forth upon [also translated as 'to
beget'] the beautiful, both in body and soul', she adds 'there's a divinity in
human propagation, an immortal something in the midst of man's mortality
which is incompatible with any discord' (*Symposium* para.206). Her

---

[21] Muir's edition of *King Lear* 4.6.161, footnote.
[22] Juliet, imagining her first embrace of Romeo, encourages herself to think that
'strange love, grown bold', when 'acted' can seem 'simple modesty' (*Romeo and
Juliet* 3.12.15). This is both an insight into a girl's fear of intercourse and her
overcoming of reluctance by thinking it as its opposite.

praise of propagation is in fact not easily reconciled with the stress on abstinence from erotic pleasures that seems to be required when she speaks of men, not women, attaining to the supreme vision. But that had been catered for in Shakespeare's day when Castiglione spoke of both women and men being capable of experiencing such a revelation.

In both Sonnets 135 and 136, 'Will' has an even greater variety of meanings than it has in earlier Sonnets in the sequence. Editors are agreed that it can mean both the male and the female sexual parts, as well as 'will' in the sense of a capacity to act on a decision, an intention, a desire or wish, and of course Shakespeare's own name: he can claim for himself both masculine and feminine gender, to be both confined in Hamlet's words, in a nutshell and yet to have a controlling power in infinite space:

> Who ever hath her wish, thou hast thy *Will*,
> And *Will* too boote, and *Will* in over-plus.
> (135.1-2)

As in the word-play on 'hence', in these words, as in all of 135 and 136, 'opposites' coincide, meaning simultaneously both. 'Whereas others have mere wishes, the mistress has an iron determination, and even more, a superlative will into the bargain and 'You have a capacity for embracing in your will with incomparable fervour' and 'you have me, your Will' with an ironical suggestion that Will finds this almost more than he can cope with:

> More then enough am I that vexe thee still,
> To thy sweet will making addition thus
> (135.3-4)

He apologises for making such demands as he made with less vigour, but equal tenderness in 'Make sweet some vial; treasure thou some place, With beauties treasure ere it be self kil'd ... (6.4). In this later Sonnet in the sequence, however, the poet is making even bolder claims:

> Wilt thou whose will is large and spatious,
> Not once vouchsafe to hide my will in thine
> (135.5-6)

It is not simply that the mistress's will, when it is called 'spatious' is 'anchor'd in the bay where all men ride' and 'the wide worlds commonplace' (137.6 and 10), though this makes her extremely promiscuous. The poet does, it is true, complain that the mistress is able to take other men into her body, whereas he is not so admitted. Yet

> The sea all water, yet receives raine still,
> And in aboundance addeth to his store
> (135.9-10)

As in Diotima's vision, the love neither waxes nor wanes, still filling with rain but contradictorily adding to an abundance; the sea is also frequently an image for love in Shakespeare. Even though the mistress is rich, she is asked by the poet to add yet one more will to the many she already admits, and all these together make her, as though she were an ocean, even more 'will' in all senses, including the forename. The couplet then presents a question for editors, who often, understandably, opt for an emendation, thus:

> Let 'no', unkind, no faire beseechers kill
> (135.13)

That is, be not so unkind as to say 'no' to fair suitors. But this requires an insertion of quotation marks and an additional comma, in place of the Quarto's

> Let no unkinde, no faire beseechers kill

'Unkind' usually means 'denying, disdaining'. The sense is that both aggressive and tender lovers are not to be allowed to destroy love; the poet in his universality includes them all:

> Thinke all [both 'unkinde' and 'fair'] but one, and me in that one *Will*
> (135.14)

Will is equally unkind and fair. One may regard this as no more than a sequence of multiple meanings using the poet's name, but this need not detract from the ambitiousness of the Sonnet as a whole: 'unkinde' and 'fair' are certainly coinciding opposites.

Sonnet 136 continues in the same vein:

> If thy soule check thee that I come so neere,
> Sweare to thy blind soule that I was thy *Will*
> (136.1-2)

There is a certain impudence in this counsel to a mistress who is, in her soul, blind, as though she could not perceive that her lover the poet was himself and no other.[23] The multiple associations of 'Will' continue in the next line:

And will thy soule knows is admitted there

as though addressing the soul rather than the body implied no offence. But that the poet speaks of the soul at all brings in clearly what had only been implied before: the love that is being spoken of is now not, or not only, a bodily love but something more akin to Diotima's vision, seen in terms of begetting.

As Colin Burrow says, the poet in the final 'Will' of the poem [135] 'becomes one universal appetitive will, uniting all lovers and the organs of both sexes into himself'.[24] The same may be said of the young man, in whose bosom reigns 'love and all love's *loving parts*' (31.3). It is equally meant for the mistress. (A parallel may also be perceived in the two gigantic figures in *Finnegans Wake*, H.C.E. Haveth Childers Everywhere and Here Comes Everybody, and his mate A.L.P.: Anna Livia Plurabelle.) This is, as it were, a 'chemical marriage', such as alchemists tried to visualize. There is both wit, ironic humour, and punning in plenty, sapping the universal implications, but these are all of a piece with the collocation of Bottom's vision with that of the poet himself in 33, and with the frequent destructive negations. The Sonnet continues:

Will will fulfill the treasure of thy love
I fill it full with wils, and my will one.
(136.5-6)

Shakespeare often puts 'I' for 'Aye', and seems to do so here. Otherwise he is assuming in himself the capacity to fill the mistress with other wills, including his own, impossible though that is, on any normal expectations. This is still all of a piece with the subsuming of his personality in a greater one. He has, after all, said that Will will do so. Editing the line as 'Aye, fill it ...' removes this audacious implication.

Yet as almost always the negation follows. The poet assumes a non-identity, 'let me passe untold [uncounted]', even though he is still 'one'. The Sonnet ends with a humble plea to be held as nothing (held in coition as in spirit), yet a nothing, in the sense of Sonnet 20.12 and 13, pleasing to the mistress. The last line is humbler still, asking merely that the poet's

---

[23] Booth, p.470.
[24] Burrow, p.650.

name be loved – and with 'for my name is *Will*' it returns simultaneously
to the proud boast – 'I am the Will that is the mistress's own will', and her
priapic counterpart. He is all and nothing.

As with the young man, there is both a cosmic allusiveness and a
mundane one. That the woman is a 'baye where all men ride' (137.6)
seems to be said disparagingly. Donne must have seen it differently when
he wrote in his Holy Sonnet XVIII of Christ's Spouse, meaning the Holy
Ghost (sometimes regarded as female) that he can scarcely believe she can
be the 'She' who has been seen in his own day in Reformation Germany,
and yet also in pre-Reformation times. 'Is she self truth and errs? Now
new outworne?' Is she already with us, or must we 'first travaile ... to
seeke and then make love?' He concludes that the wife of Christ can
resemble a profligate:

> Betray kind husband [Christ] thy spouse to our sights,
> And let myne amorous soule court thy mild Dove,
> Who is most trew, and pleasing to thee, then
> When she is embraced and open to most men.

The meaning is spiritual and mystical, as in Christian interpretations of the
erotic *Song of Solomon* regarded as a love-poem between the Church and
the individual soul. Shakespeare is more critical, and more ambiguous.
For him, or rather for the Sonnets poet, the mistress is 'the wide worlds
common place' (137.10), and he is corrupted when he seeks her otherwise.
There is, no doubt, a double meaning once again, if 'common place' means
a place where all may meet together, but it may also be taken to mean love
is a commonplace, it is what everyone enjoys, and none the worse for that.

To stress that all this is implied by no more than playing on the name of
Will is to belittle it, as it no doubt deserves. Yet also this word-play is
better understood in terms of Cleopatra's praise of Antony, and the huge
implications of the poet's love for the young man: they are impossible, yet
meant with great insistence by Shakespeare as by her. (In the Sonnet, it
may be seen for a moment, there is only the *wish* to be accepted, not the
reality. But it is a wish made by the Will itself, who has already accepted.)
To claim that by virtue of a forename one is supreme in will is absurd. But
Shakespeare felt his power to create dramas and poems to be
immeasurable. He was encouraged by it and humbled. There is no need to
take these two Sonnets only for what they say, without regard to the unique
imagination with which he was endowed.

Certainly there are passages in the plays where promiscuousness is seen
with horror. Othello torments himself with the thought that Desdemona
might be available to all:

I had been happy if the general camp
Pioners [labourers] and all, had tasted her sweet body,
So I had nothing known.
(*Othello* 3.3.342-3)

In *Troilus* there is as near an approximation to such a scene as Othello
imagines, so far as the theatre allows, when 'general' Agamemnon kisses
Cressida, and Ulysses remarks,

> Twere better she were kissed in general [generally]

and when after another all the Greeks of rank kiss her, giving Ulysses
cause to say

> Her wanton spirits look out
> At every joint and motive [moving part] of her body.
> (*T. and C.* 4.5.18-63)

The scene is almost a realisation of what Othello liked to imagine, and
there is no attempt at justifying Cressida.   In fact it only reinforces the
sickened diatribe of Troilus when he sees her as one of the 'daughters of
the game', in Ulysses' words.

At the other extreme is the delectable moment in the Epilogue of *As
You Like It* when Rosalind steps forward to tease the men in the audience
with their affection towards their wives, and to say that if she were a
woman – but as they know, she is a boy – she would 'kiss as many of you
as had beards that pleased me, complexions that liked me, and breaths that
I defied [disliked] not …', which must account for a good few.   It is an
offer Orlando would not approve of, if he were there, but then it is also not
really an offer, in so far as it is made by the boy actor, merely a delightful
thought to send the men in the audience home with.   At the same time it is
the corresponding moment to the cosmic love of the mistress in Sonnets
135-136.   As in *A Midsummer Night's Dream*, and in *The Merchant of
Venice*, the last words of the play evoke pleasing thoughts of happiness in
bed, the kind of happiness Donne celebrated when he was young.   (A
contrasting opposite is the Epilogue of *Troilus and Cressida* where
Pandarus appears to accuse the entire audience in the theatre of unbridled
lechery, and wishes they may all catch syphilis.)

Inevitably, there is a withdrawal.   The poet asks whether it is 'Alcumie'
that is making 'monsters and things indigest Such cherubines as your sweet
selfe resemble' (114.4-6).   There is no end to the opposites.

The Sonnets conclude with the two versions of the poem by Marianus Scholasticus[25], in an entirely different style from all the rest, narrating the tale of Cupid's fire being taken to provide heat for a healing bath. The tale varies only a little in each case, but each reaffirms love in the strongest terms. The poet was not cured by the bath, but turns again to the mistress:

> But found no cure, the bath for my helpe lies,
> Where *Cupid* got new fire: my mistres eye.
> (153.13-14)

It has been suggested that the bath that failed was one that cured venereal disease,[26] from which the poet was suffering, and which failed to cure him. Even if this is so, which is doubtful, his resolution is unaffected. It is worth while to love, even with such a risk. In the last Sonnet of all, it is not clearly said that the poet was not cured, but the couplet is as positive as the preceding one with its allusion to the *Song of Solomon* (8.6-7) 'many waters cannot quench love':

> Came there for cure and this by that I prove,
> Loves fire heates water, water cooles not love.
> (154.13-14)

These two distinctive poems with their similar contents, are like the couplet that ends a scene or an act, marking a final moment. The Sonnets conclude with a defiant reassertion of love as always triumphant, even a love as 'diseased' as this.

Donne is clearer in exploring the contradictions of love than Shakespeare is, but then he does not embrace them so wholeheartedly, in all their confusion of identities. Throughout the Sonnets the help to understanding is that, as in Sonnet 116, any deviation from love on account of some change or changed perception, means an end to love. The poet maintains an unchanging, universal love (124.5 and 11) by offering a defence of the lover or the mistress that is untenable and yet to all appearances sincere. He sins by loving, but love remains intact. We shall meet a remarkable instance of this in Desdemona's reply to Othello as he demands that she thinks on the sins he supposes her to have committed.

---

[25] Kerrigan, p.422.

[26] See Duncan-Jones, p.422; Kerrigan, p.423; Burrow, p.686; and James Dutton, 'Analogues of Shakespeare's Sonnets 153-4', *Modern Philology* 38 (1941), pp.385-400.

*   *   *   *   *

Baudelaire's love for the mulatto woman Jeanne Duval, as described by
Enid Starkie, reflects closely the love of the Sonnets poet for the black
mistress, his *Vénus noire*, although Baudelaire seems to have had little
more than a general appreciation of Shakespeare, and would scarcely have
wanted to imitate him. He could be exasperated beyond the pitch of
endurance by some cruelty, treachery or errant stupidity on her part. She
was not, others said, beautiful, though one friend saw something divine
in her as well as bestial, and Baudelaire adored her for her beauty.
Imperturbable, she would listen to his protestations of love, placidly
reclining in her armchair, utterly remote. Yet love, for him, was first a
longing for perfect beauty, and he loved the human body because it seemed
to him to be the concrete and material expression of the divine. He would
have fervently kissed her '*noble corps*' if she had made the least
welcoming gesture, even if only to 'obscurir la splendeur de tes froides
prunelles' 'to hide the splendour of your cold pupils'. Though their
relationship cooled, for the rest of his life he remained bound to her by ties
of loyalty, sympathy and even of affection:

> Et je chéris, ô bête implacable et cruelle
> Jusqu'à cette froideur par où tu m'es plus belle.

> And I cherish, O implacable and cruel monster, even that coldness that
> makes you for me all the more beautiful.

These lines are close to those of several Sonnets, in which Shakespeare
professes his love for the mistress not in spite of but because of the faults
that are so clearly apparent.

The similarity appears the greater when one considers how both
Baudelaire and Shakespeare speak of this love in relation to some divine
quality, even though this may also be far from divine:

> Viens-tu du ciel profond ou sors-tu de l'abîme,
> Ô Beauté? ton regard, infernal et divin,
> Verse confusément le bienfait et le crime,
> Et l'on peut pour cela te comparer au vin.

> Are you from the deep sky or from the abyss, O Beauty? your look,
> infernal and divine, confounds both good and evil, and for this we may
> compare you to wine.

Similarly the black mistress sometimes appears to the poet as though she had come from hell. The possibility that she was a real woman in a real relationship is strengthened by the comparison.

François Truffaut's famous film *Jules et Jim* has a brief discussion of Baudelaire and his attitude to women. It also matches the Sonnets theme, two devoted lovers in love with the same woman, who literally drives one of them to death. Shakespeare's name is mentioned twice as though drawing discreet attention to the similarity.

CHAPTER THREE

THE SONNETS AND THE PLAYS

Whenever there was an opportunity, Shakespeare converted or adapted a plot so as to reflect in some degree themes of the Sonnets. In many of the comedies and in some of the tragedies too, there is a pair of friends, or close acquaintances, one of whom suspects the other of having an affair with his wife or mistress, and in other plays, while there is no such jealousy, the pair of friends and the mistress remain. In the earliest plays, the reminiscences of the Sonnets are clearer. *Two Gentlemen of Verona* could have been written to dramatise the Sonnets – Valentine and Proteus correspond better than any other pair to his poet and his lover, even to the point that Valentine yields his mistress to Proteus in the generous spirit of Sonnet 40 ('Take all my loves ...'). In *A Midsummer Night's Dream* Demetrius and Lysander are transformed by Puck's magic into rivals in love, and in *The Merchant of Venice* Antonio and Bassanio are devoted friends, though not both in love with the same woman. Antony and Enobarbus are friends, though not on the same footing, and Enobarbus's admiration for Cleopatra does not amount to love. Hamlet and Horatio are close to one another, but Horatio has scarcely any awareness of Ophelia at all. Cassio is a friend of Othello, suspected of having an affair with Desdemona, who like Ophelia is innocent of the charges brought against her. In fact the 'black' mistress of the Sonnets seldom turns up in the plays as an unfaithful woman. Cressida is almost the only one, for Cleopatra's affairs are long past, and Antony has rather her apparent indifference than any infidelity to meet with love. In the later plays the suspected woman is always innocent, though her husband or lover is convinced of the contrary. Mariana, Hero, Hermione, Imogen, and the virgin Marina all represent what the Sonnets poet sees in his unfaithful mistress, but are exonerated, sometimes movingly, as when Hermione suddenly becomes alive. The male-female figure of Sonnets 20 and 53 is mirrored in Proteus's Julia, Portia, Rosalind, Viola and Imogen, and the list ends with the last play, *The Two Noble Kinsmen*, returning to the Palamon and Arcite of Chaucer's Knight's Tale, both in love with Emilia. Shakespeare constantly tries to build into the plays some aspect of the Sonnets. Some passages are illuminated by these resemblances.

In *Twelfth Night* Orsino plays in Shakespeare's imagination the role of the Sonnets poet. He is in love with Olivia, who fits into the dramatist's pattern by means of an ingenious triviality. In the Sonnets the mistress is frequently called 'black', often in a moral sense. In Sonnet 127, the mistress's eyes are 'Raven blacke', not indicating any lack of virtue but as mourners who are saddened by other women's use of cosmetics, disgracing their natural beauty, and this makes them even more attractive to the Sonnets poet. So beautiful are they that 'every toung saies beauty should look so' (127.14). This is the meaning of a later Sonnet: 'all my best doth worship thy defect' (149.11) and 'in my minde thy worst all best exceeds' (150.9), but the moral is applied without regard to content: mourning eyes are greeted in the same way as 'black' conduct. And so for the plot of *Twelfth Night* it is enough for Olivia to be black in mourning for her brother. The parallel with the Sonnets poet and the black mistress is in Shakespeare's eyes, and, in so far as it enables him to forward the plot, but is enough for practical purposes. It remains only for Orsino to realise that the boy he sent to woo Olivia is his master-mistress, and can return his love as a woman should.

A single word shows Shakespeare's mind at work as he brings Sonnets and plays together. When Olivia, impressed by the boldness of the 'boy' Viola, come to woo her on Orsino's behalf, she asks him how he would woo her on his own behalf, if asked to do so. Viola replies that she would 'hallow your name', but Shakespeare at once realises as he writes that such language is that of the Sonnets poet when, 'like prayers divine', he first 'hallowed your fair name' (108.5 and 8). This devotion will not do, in the play, and he adds the words, making ordinary sense after all 'your name to the reverberate hills' (*T.N.* 1.5.280 Folio). 'Hallow' becomes 'halloo' or 'hallo', and is so printed by editors. The momentary identity of Viola and the Sonnets mistress is swept aside, together with Shakespeare's personal involvement.

Sonnets 133 and 134 accuse the mistress of being a usurer, who 'put'st forth all to use'; she has made a slave of the lover, and imprisoned him in her steel bosom. His lover wrote 'suretie-like' on the poet's behalf, and she will now 'sue a friend come debter for my sake' (134.11). He pays the whole, and yet the poet is not free. Writing these lines, Shakespeare clearly had in mind Shylock and Antonio's bond, fitting the metaphors as closely as he could to the circumstances of the play. *The Merchant of Venice* was in fact ideally suited to his continual wish to write plays at least alluding to the Sonnets poet and his lover, and their mistress. His source on this occasion, *Il Pecorone*, afforded the whole story, including a

Shylock and a Portia, who comes from Belmont, as in the play, to plead on
Antonio's behalf. Antonio and Bassanio, however, are in the Italian
version a godfather and a godson. By turning them into two devoted
lovers Shakespeare at once made a much more dramatic confrontation
possible, as well as achieving his aim of bringing in the Sonnets. No better
opportunity had ever been afforded so far, to show the willingness to
sacrifice himself of one of the lovers for the other. When Antonio bares
his breast for Shylock's knife he is almost a Christ-like figure, bearing the
agony on his friend's behalf without a murmur of complaint, bearing it out
even to the edge of doom, 'the coward conquest of a wretches knife'
(74.11). For Shakespeare the courtroom scene must have been exquisitely
painful to write, enacting what the Sonnets could only say in words, his
willingness to suffer for his love.

Antonio is not in love with Portia; he is no rival to Bassanio as he
would have been if the Sonnets story-line had been adhered to completely.
This would have detracted from the immediate impact of the scene. Portia,
however, praises him in the highest degree, as though she were almost in
love with him. Since he and Bassanio 'bear an egal yoke of love', there
must needs be 'a like proportion of lineaments, of manners, and of spirit'

Which makes me think that this Antonio,
Being the bosom lover of my lord,
Must needs be like my lord. If it be so,
How little is the cost I have bestowed
In purchasing the semblance of my soul
From out the state of hellish cruelty
(*Merchant of Venice* 3.4.13-21)

By 'the semblance of my soul' she means Antonio. Shakespeare could go
no closer than this to hint at a lover's relationship between all three, while
still leaving Antonio separated from the other two.

Portia's disguise as a young man suits her perfectly for the role of
male-female ideal figure, as in Sonnet 20. Through her, however, we
broach the much greater issues presented by the play. In broad strokes *The
Merchant* presents the contrast of Jew and Christian as it was and still is
perceived by many Christians, the Jew standing for strict adherence to the
letter of the law, the Christian for grace, mercy and loving kindness. Never
mind that the God of the Old Testament is sometimes merciful. The
contrast is established and would certainly have been understood as true by
spectators at the original performances of the play. Shakespeare, of
course, while adhering to the main thrust of the anti-Jewish story, supplies
speeches in which Shylock is made more intelligible: Antonio has spat on
him and his daughter has run away with a Christian. He expects no fair

play from the court, and above all, he has been given the great speech asking how a Jew differs from a Christian in his basic human qualities. Such a speech could only have been written in the consciousness of the universal love to which Shakespeare commits himself in Sonnets 116 and 124. The same is true of the speech in which Shylock tells the Duke, in the presence of the whole court, that he is arbitrary in justifying to himself the use of slaves. An anti-slavery speech at such an early stage in European history is innovative, and again one senses that Shakespeare was inspired by his great ideal. Portia's speech, 'The quality of mercy' is likewise explicable only in such terms.

But there is a qualification in these instances. Shylock's demand that Christians should recognise him as a human being turns at the end of the speech to an unexpected conclusion.

> If a Christian wrong a Jew, what should his sufferance be by Christian
> example? Why revenge!
> (*Merchant of Venice* 3.1.65-6)

and when he confronts the Duke with his unwillingness to let his children marry his slaves (*Merchant of Venice* 4.1.90-103) he does so only to defend his own arbitrary behaviour in demanding his pound of flesh. Neither speech is really concerned with love.

Portia's speech is in itself above such criticism. It presents mercy in the highest terms imaginable – mightiest in the mightiest, the attribute to awe and majority, an attribute to God Himself – and at the same time beyond the power of ordinary mortals to truly display. 'In the course of justice none of us should see salvation' (*Merchant of Venice* 4.1.102-3). But when her plea fails, when Shylock continues unmoved to sharpen his knife, she and all the rest of those present forget mercy and press for the severest penalties, Shylock has no conceivable defence. He has behaved abominably. Antonio is lucky to be alive. Yet when the Duke has spared his life, granting half his wealth to Antonio, the other half going to the 'general state', and when Portia asks Antonio what mercy he can show, there is little mercy to be had from the Christians. Antonio has suffered in the extreme. He has also despised Shylock from the outset. He is in no state of mind to weigh calmly what he does when he offers to restore the fine for one half of Shylock's goods, the other half to be kept in trust for Shylock's daughter's Christian husband – but all on condition that he becomes a Christian. 'Art thou contented, Jew?', Portia asks, using in merciless scorn the name by which he has been more and more addressed during the court proceedings.

This could have seemed to Shakespeare's audiences a fair conclusion. It is hard to see how Shakespeare's vision of universal love could have borne it. Jews had been compelled to convert to Christianity, or be expelled, a hundred years before, in the Spain of Ferdinand and Isabella. In Jonathan Miller's production a bystander took off the chain round his neck and pressed the crucifix hanging from it to Shylock's lips. It is a vivid illustration of what devastation this must cause, what total affliction. He of course has no defence, no means of justifying himself after his monstrous actions. But mercy would not have pressed so far, and Shakespeare knew that. Antonio's demand, though justifiable to him and in the eyes of many Christians of his time, has to be seen in the light of the humanity to which Shylock had already drawn our attention. After this, the remainder of the play is in a different key.

The moonlit night at Belmont, celebrated by the two young lovers, is one of the most wonderfully beautiful scenes Shakespeare or anyone else ever wrote. It is followed by the return of Portia and the teasing of Bassanio and Gratiano by her and Nerissa, ending with a promise after all, that love will transform the night for them too. Shylock is totally forgotten. This is the ending of the play on a Sonnets theme with which it all began. Can the failure of mercy in the final moments of the trial-scene have been a mere interruption? It may be a good enough answer to propose that Shakespeare was content to have made the presence of mercy, and of humanity and equality felt, feeling he could do no more. He had provided a work which would certainly satisfy the ages-old anti-Semitism of his time. The audience would certainly see the knife-flourishing Shylock confronting the bare-breasted Antonio, his arms held horizontally by his friends as though in crucifixion, as the very image of 'the Jew who killed Christ'. That was how the trial had to end. But for him, Antonio was himself, willing to die for his lover. He could only, after that, return to the play he had meant to write in the first place, and celebrate the love not only between the principals, but between the servants as well. The ecstasy of the moonlit night belongs to that play, not to the play that had broken into what he had intended.

Revenge is alien to the Sonnets. *Hamlet* was oriented quite differently, yet the detestation of women, corresponding especially to some of the Sonnets to or about the black mistress, was aptly displayed in the diatribe against Ophelia. Hamlet does not dwell on it, though it is in his mind again when he denounces Gertrude's infidelity. He scarcely thinks of Ophelia until he jumps into her grave, protesting a love for her beyond any that Laertes can imagine. We have no need to doubt him, but the combined hatred and love is better understood in the Sonnets.

As You Like It offered the Sonnets poet much more. Not only is he present in Orlando, attaching his sonnets to trees, but of course in Rosalind. When she calls herself Ganymede, using the name of the youth loved by Zeus, and when she, in reality a boy-actor, pretends to be a girl who pretends to be a boy who offers to let Orlando woo her as a woman, the master-mistress is presented for the first time without disguise. The 'opposites' play their part in the scene where the other young lovers protest their love in a charming sequence of short lines, only to be compared by Rosalind with the howling of Irish wolves. Country manners and courtiers' niceties are contrasted in the scene where Corin and Touchstone confront each other — contrasted, rather than presented as opposites. Touchstone's love of Audrey, however, is another matter. It has been observed by Katherine Duncan-Jones that Sonnet 130, with its refusal to compare the mistress's eyes with the sun, its description of her hair as wires, its dislike of her bad breath, and yet its protestation of love for her nevertheless, is not simply a satire on the extravagant praises afforded by poets to their lady loves. It, she observes, 'strongly parallels Touchstone's wooing of the honestly ugly and wanton Audrey' (*As You Like It* 3.3.1-57). That is to say, Audrey corresponds in this to the black mistress. The mistress, it is true, is never spoken of in such gross terms as Touchstone uses, not of Audrey but of the girl he says he loved before he met her: 'I remember the kissing of her batlet [wooden paddle for washing clothes] and the cow's dugs that her pretty chopt [chapped] hands had milked' (*A.Y.L.I.* 2.2.45-50). These are satirical certainly, but they also show, if you will, what a truly universal love would need to encompass. (In Christian terms rather than erotic ones, there is a parallel with saints like St Elizabeth of Hungary, who kissed grisly wounds out of compassion.) Touchstone and Audrey stand together in the concluding wedding ceremonies, alongside Orlando and Rosalind as the lovers who are not in the least spiritual, but welcome love of the body – however gross – just as much.

In a final opposition, Jaques turns his back on the whole company, though wishing them well, and retires to a convent, joining the Duke to 'put on a religious life' (*A.Y.L.I.* 5.4.181). The whole pastoral world is negated. The title of the play itself can be understood both as affirming: 'this is just the thing for you', and denying: 'This is the kind of thing you like'.

Othello is at once the Sonnets-poet, in so far as he shares the poet's suspicions of women, and, being black, the mistress, at least as Desdemona learns to see him. The play would, however, be too stark an image of marital jealousy were it not for the words spoken, all too briefly, by Desdemona as she confronts his murderous intention. She is to be blamed for her inaction, for not crying out for help, but she has means of her own for confronting death. What Othello demands that she think on her sins, she replies:

They are loves I bear to you.
(*Othello* 5.2.40)

She does not simply admit having sinned, although in Othello's sense she has never done so, never been unfaithful or disloyal. She may think her disobedience towards her father was sinful, as a woman of her time might well do. But whatever sins she has in mind, she neither admits nor defends herself. Her sins *are* loves she 'bears' to him as a wife might bear her husband's child, or carry her loves towards him. This is a perfect example of the combination of opposites, in that neither the loves nor the sins are denied, while also neither is affirmed except in terms of the other. The Sonnets-poet thinks similarly when he says he is both adversary and advocate of his love.

There is no place for the Sonnets-poet in *King Lear*. No lovers, no reconciliations, no fusions, the play moves relentlessly to the bleak ending, when by mere chance Cordelia is not saved from hanging, and Lear is left with the vain hope that she still breathes. The play is remarkable, however, for the fact that the sub-plot so closely resembles the main plot. In both plots an old man is hounded by a child or children, though defended so far as possible by one child. The circumstances of their end are different. Lear has lost Cordelia, Gloucester's son Edgar has been restored to him. There is just reason, then, for the way in which Edgar reports his father's death:

> I asked his blessing, and from first to last
> Told him our pilgrimage. But his flawed heart –
> Alack, too weak the conflict to support –
> 'Twixt two extremes of passion, joy and grief
> *Burst smilingly.*
> (*K.L.* 5.3.197-201)

There was no such release for Lear. The loving opposition of the Fool could not be sustained. But the fashioning of the sub-plot so closely to Lear's own suggests an intention on Shakespeare's part to present a different, though not an alternative ending. The parallel narrative, like that of *A Lover's Complaint*, presents an opposite against which the starkest tragic ending can be reflected, though not denied.

Grudin's interpretation (p.142) would see the whole of *King Lear* as a circle of opposites with Lear, Gloucester and the Fool in the middle. This is easily seen in the opposites Edgar and Edmund, Cordelia and Goneril or Regan, but Albany is not opposite to Cornwall, nor is Burgundy opposite to France. The serving-man who protests at the blinding of Gloucester does not appear in Grudin's circle, yet his humanity carries great weight.

The fact that the good (on the whole) confront the evil needs no philosophy of opposites to make it plain.

Troilus and Cressida begins as though alluding to the first seventeen Sonnets, in which the poet urges the young man to beget children. Pandarus's encouragement of the two young lovers is of a different kind. He relishes the implied analogy between kneading bread and fondling Cressida, waiting for the right moment, heating up, and other processes of cooking, and though avuncular in a not very caring way, is a complete contrast to the poet whose only concern is that beauty should be preserved in future generations. But there is not enough matter here for a whole play, and we turn to the long debates and discussions in the Greek camp, and the justified attacks by Thersites on the shame of wars and lechery. When the abrupt demand arrives, that Cressida leave Troy in order to be the wife of Diomedes, in exchange for Antenor, she is still innocent, and hardly to be blamed as Troilus blames her for deserting him. He does not intervene on her behalf, yielding to necessity, while she, first kissed by all the Greek leaders and then consigned to Diomedes, resigns herself to a life of subservience that she can only endure by offering love of some sort to her conqueror. Yet the situation is there, as in the Sonnets about the black mistress. Troilus tries to cope, seeing Cressida in a dual light, and in doing so rejects the whole philosophy of reconciling opposites:

> O madness of discourse,
> That cause sets up with and against itself:
> Bifold authority, where reason can revolt
> Without perdition, and loss assume all reason
> Without revolt. This is, and is not Cressid.
> Within my soul there doth conduce a fight
> Of this strange nature, that a thing inseparable
> Divides more widely than the sun and earth;
> And yet the spacious breadth of this division
> Admits no orifex [opening] for a point as subtle
> As Ariachne's broken woof to enter.
> (*Troilus and Cressida* 5.2.140-150)

Desdemona, the Sonnets-poet, and a whole traditional school of philosophers from Heraclitus onward could accept these paradoxes. Troilus can't, and Shakespeare shows his independence of the tradition in writing these lines for him. Reason seemed less important in 'The Phoenix and the Turtle':

> Reason, in itself confounded,
> Saw division grow together,
> To themselves yet either neither,

Simple were so well confounded;
That it cried 'How true a twain
Seemeth this concordant one!
Love hath reason, reason none,
If what parts can so remain.
(*The Phoenix and the Turtle* 41-49)

Shakespeare can take both sides, adopting the paradoxes and yet rejecting them. Troilus, bereft of love, can only turn to bitter hatred.

Yet in *Antony and Cleopatra* he returns to paradox throughout the play; in fact, this is the positive to the negative of *Troilus*. In a sense, the polarities have not been abandoned even as they are, in *Troilus*, rejected. So long as they continue to be used, it can be argued that rejecting them is merely part of the dialectic, that they are still, as a system, operative over against their rejection.

Two plays that stand out from the rest are *Measure for Measure* and *The Tempest*. In each of them the plot concerns an attempt by someone with power to bring home their sins to one or more people, ending with a degree of self-knowledge and repentance. None of the other plays have any such concern, and these two stand out as having no interest in ambiguities, except to question them. (See Chapter Four.)

Measure for Measure, it is true, has recently been interpreted by Nuttall in the light of the ideas of an obscure early Christian sect, the Ophite Gnostics, and those of Luther and Calvin. 'Shakespeare', he writes, 'gives us a redemption in which the demonized Angelo is the Christ-figure'.

In terms of Ophite Gnosticism 'God is a jealous, punitive figure and the snake [in the Garden of Eden] his noble antagonist, the champion of humanity'. And 'the serpent is Christ'. In Calvinistic terms, as defined here, Jesus in atoning for mankind commits all possible sins, thus bearing the consequences of all mankind's sins. Luther believed Christ committed the worst sins of all, he despaired and 'the humiliation of Christ is absolute' (p.264).

The resemblance between these views and those of philosophers of dialectical opposites and coincidence is apparent. But that leaves the interpretation of *Measure for Measure* still to be made, and there are serious obstacles. It is not true that 'Shakespeare gives us a redemption in which the demonized Angelo is the Christ-figure' (p.274). Angelo is not demonized. Entrusted with applying the law with greater severity than the Duke had done, he condemns Claudio to death for adultery. There is no crime or sin in that, but he blackmails Isabella into consenting to accept him in bed, promising to release Claudio, her brother. Even when he thinks, falsely, that he has had her in sexual intercourse, he does not release Claudio. When challenged by Mariana, who substituted for Isabella, he does not scruple to denounce her for adultery. Only at the very last, when he is cornered, does he confess and repent, and that repentance looks suspect in the circumstances.

Nuttall says of the blackmailing that it is of no importance in 'the heretical paradox of the play'; it is merely 'necessary to the comedy of the plot'. Shakespeare 'undoubtedly feels with Angelo'. But this is a Christ-figure who is wholly self-seeking. He is called Angelo ironically, not because Isabella says 'You bid me seek redemption of the devil' (5.1.29), as though she were unconsciously speaking the truth. Angelo does not 'take upon his shoulders the burden of sin so that we can be happy' (p.269). He loves nobody. Nuttall is misled by the analogous inversions of Michel Foucault, whom he acknowledges at the end of his account.

Shakespeare's version suffers, as a play about mercy and justice, from the intrigue that begins when the Duke returns and learns of Angelo's proposal to Isabella. All he needs to do in order to prevent any injustice to Claudio is to reveal himself and remove Angelo from power. Instead, he prolongs the play by his proposal that Isabella should pretend to agree to Angelo's demand, that Mariana should also agree to accept what he intends as rape, and thereby secure him as a husband. To stave off execution, the grisly business of substituting a head for Claudio's involves postponing the beheading of Barnardine on the grounds that he is too drunk to lose his life at the moment, and the fortunate discovery that the head of Ragozine is available instead. This provides dramatic suspense, but in the final scene, where a kind of Last Judgment is enacted with the Duke acting 'like power divine' (*M. for M.* 5.1.374). A whole series of judgements are passed, only to be rescinded because in fact Angelo has neither raped Isabella nor caused the death of Claudio.

Angelo is sentenced, as a 'measure for measure', as though he really had had Claudio executed. But this would be unfair: the Duke left Angelo in power precisely so that he should be stricter than he had been himself, and bears some responsibility for having done so. The blackmailing of Isabella is never punished as such. Finally, in a scene of general pardon, one that can well have appealed to Shakespeare's forgiving nature, especially bearing in mind his attachment to a universal love, marriages are arranged in a way too much like a conventional theatrical final curtain, where the actors take hands and advance towards the audience, accepting their applause. Mariana may be glad to welcome Angelo as her husband: it is not at all clear that Angelo will feel the same. He has rejected her on grounds of her supposed infidelity only a moment ago. The Duke's offer of marriage to Isabella, who till this moment has expected to begin a life of complete chastity, is too sudden, although on stage Isabella may be allowed a moment of deep reflection. She never accepts. Barnardine the murderer is pardoned without more ado, but Lucio is condemned to marry a prostitute who is now said to be with child by him on the grounds that he has 'slandered a prince', namely the Duke, despite the fact that he spoke up boldly against Angelo, encouraging Isabella to go on with her demand for Claudio's warrant to be annulled. It would all sound much better as a demonstration of belief in mercy if it were not for these devices, adopting too closely the story of the earlier play.

In *The Tempest* Shakespeare again writes a play in which wrongdoers are brought to book. Again, it is not based on paradox, and yet paradox plays an important part through the character of Gonzalo, the one courtier in Alfonso's retinue who is not like the rest. He alone, rather like the Banished Duke in *As You Like* It, who sees 'good in everything', sees the island on which they are all shipwrecked as beautiful, having 'everything advantageous to life'; for him the grass is lush and lusty, the clothes they wear, despite the shipwreck, are fresh as though new-dyed (the Sonnets poet takes the worst and sees it, with love, as best (137.4)), and he is mocked by Adrian and Sebastian for his credulity (*T.* 2.1.37-100). In his Utopia all the women are pure, the people innocent (*T.* 2.1.169) and he would govern it 't'excel the Golden Age'. The inhabitants of the island are paradoxically 'though of monstrous shape', 'more gentle, kind, than of our human generation you shall find many – nay almost any', and for this, he is called by Prospero, overhearing him, 'honest lord' (*T.* 2.3.31-35). Later, he is for Prospero a 'noble friend' (*T.* 5.1.120) even 'Holy Gonzalo, 'honourable man' (*T.* 5.1.62); for him Prospero feels great sympathy:

> Mine eyes, even sociable to the show of thine,
> Fall fellowly drops.
> (*T.* 5.1.62-3)

In all these ways Prospero acknowledges Gonzalo's virtue in seeing good where others see evil. This is, after all, an island which even Caliban finds 'full of sweet airs', though the Bermudas, presumably the islands in Shakespeare's imagination, were known as an Isle of Devils. Miranda, inspired by love of Ferdinand, sees only a 'brave new world, that has such people in it' (*T.* 5.1.183), and Prospero goes along with her to the extent that it is new to her. Somewhere in the background lies the thought expressed in the Sonnets, that love can deceive: 'Thou blinde foole love, what doost thou to mine eyes, That they behold and see not what they see … (137.1-2) and 'O me! what eyes hath love put in my head, Which have no correspondence with true sight' (148.1-2). Prospero never speaks so critically of Gonzalo's vision or Miranda's love; he has in fact great sympathy for both, but his actions are closer to those of some pagan or Old

Testament god, raising storms, visiting ghastly pains on some of the wrongdoers, even pursuing them with spirits in the shape of dogs and hounds. His purpose is merciful, but it renounces all concern with gentle persuasion. Even as he summons up the shapes of goddesses and nymphs to celebrate the nuptials of Ferdinand and Miranda, he becomes aware of Caliban's plot against his life, breaks off, and turns to magic one last time. Caliban is a devil, 'a born devil' on whom his pains though 'humanely taken', are 'all, all lost, quite lost!' (*T.* 4.1.188-190). Only violence can meet the threat. Gonzalo's innocence, admirable though it is, is rejected along with the idea that love can transform. Only after this can Prospero return to his earlier self:

> *Ariel:*Your charm so strongly works
>   That if you now beheld them, your affections
>   would become tender.
> *Prospero:*   Dost thou think so, spirit?
> *Ariel:*Mine would, sir, were I human
> *Prospero:*   And mine shall.
> (*T.* 5.1.17-19)

The rarer action is in virtue than in vengeance. Humanity returns, but not paradoxically, only as a recognition of its superior quality. On these terms the play can move to its conclusion, the wrongdoers (mostly) now repentant, the former order restored, a happy marriage for the young couple in prospect, with Prospero finally humble in his appeal to the audience for their prayers.

Of the later plays there is little to say that is relevant to the Sonnets or to the themes based on them. *Cymbeline* of course has the familiar plot concerning a jealous husband's suspicions of his innocent wife, but in addition Imogen is a master-mistress in her disguise as a man, adored by the two brothers – not simply close friends, who act out a little play within the play, with little connection with the main plot, and closer to the Sonnets situation. *The Winter's Tale* has just the jealousy of Leontes and his suspicion of his close friend Polixenes. *The Two Noble Kinsmen* closely resembles the *Two Gentlemen of Verona*, but is this time a direct dramatisation of Chaucer's tale of Palamon and Arcite, two close friends in love with Emilia. *Cardenio*, the 'lost' play based on a story in *Don Quixote*, is again about two friends in love with the same woman, though this says nothing about whether Shakespeare had any part in the play *Double Falsehood*, based on *Cardenio*, which certainly has that same theme. The compulsion to go on envisaging if not writing a play on the 'Sonnets theme' continues to the very last.

CHAPTER FOUR

THE SONNETS
AND *ANTONY AND CLEOPATRA*

It must have seemed, when Shakespeare came across Plutarch's *Life*, that his earliest attempts at working in some reference to the Sonnets were now capable of being realised almost to the full. There are no rival lovers in the play, but Enobarbus is at the least a great admirer of Cleopatra, and devoted to Antony as well as a boon companion, even after his disillusionment. He dies of shame at forsaking his master. The queen herself is the black mistress, making credible what is often merely asserted in the poems. Her treatment of Antony is sometimes harsh in the extreme. The message that she is dead, with the request to be told how he takes the news, deals a more devastating blow than any given by the black mistress of the Sonnets, leading him to kill himself. Yet Antony, humiliated by her flight from battle and by his own loss of soldierly honour, still loves as much as the Sonnets poet does, as much as Desdemona loves Othello. That the resemblance with the Sonnets is intentional is shown by Cleopatra's description of herself as 'black' with the sun's rays (*A. and C.* 1.5.280): the word is used in other plays with just such an implication, though without such a realisation.

There are more resemblances than this. When Cleopatra speaks of Antony's 'bounty', that was 'an autumn, That grew the more by reaping' (5.2.87-8) she repeats the thought that the lover's 'bountie' appears in the 'foyzon [harvest] of the year' (53.9-12). Her self-defence, that 'we, the greatest, are misthought For things that others do' (5.2.176-7) resembles the poet's refusal to be judged by others' standards ('they that levell At my abuses, reckon up their owne' (121.9-10)). She is little different from the woman who is 'the baye where all men ride' (137.6), although only the best would suit her.

Shakespeare's imagination is at work in both the Sonnets and the play, using an image belonging equally to both. It may even appear that several Sonnets were written with the play rather than personal experience in mind. When the Sonnets lover asks 'wherefore say not I that I am old?'

(138.10), implying that the mistress also is old and that she lies about it (138.12), he momentarily looks more like Antony than himself, though other Sonnets also mention the poet's age. 'Therefore I lye with her, and she with me, And in our faults by lyes we flattered be' (138.13-14) fits the play very well, and Antony's desperate attempt at breaking away from Cleopatra is echoed in 'Past cure I am, now Reason is past care, And frantick madde with ever-more unrest' (147.9-10). His time-worn declaration that he is with her even when absent (1.4.4-5) is better expressed in the Sonnet ending 'And that thou teachest how to make one twaine, By praising him here who doth hence remaine' (39.13-14), with its ambiguous 'hence' (as argued earlier). The poet's assurance that he is right to love his mistress, despite qualms, because his 'flesh ... rising at thy name doth point out thee' (150.8-9) is just the kind of argument Antony might accept when he returns to Cleopatra even after she has deceived him with the message she is dead. Her attraction to him is erotically irresistible.

These are isolated comparisons. A theme that is found in the Sonnets is the praise of the lover as 'lascivious grace in whom all il wel showes' (40.13): both well and simultaneously showing its ill, while the mistress has 'this becomming of things il' (150.5). Something similar is often said both of Cleopatra and Antony. It is part of the process by which the audience is helped to feel reconciled with and even to admire their great erotic love. 'Fie, wrangling queen', Antony says, 'Whom everything becomes – to chide, to laugh, to weep; whose every passion fully [absolutely, successfully] strives to make itself, in thee, fair and admired' (1.1.48-49). Cleopatra says of him 'Be'st thou sad or merry, The violence of either thee becomes, So does it no man else' (1.5.59-60). Enobarbus remembers when Cleopatra was out of breath, and when she spoke 'did make defect perfection (2.2.236-7) (compare 'all my best doth worship thy defect' (149.11)); adding

> other women cloy
> The appetites they feed, but she makes hungry
> Where most she satisfies; for vilest things
> *Become themselves in* her, that the holy priests
> Bless her when she is riggish [randy]
> (2.2.242-46)

There can be no doubt that Shakespeare was expanding in the play ideas that had no substantiation in the Sonnets, being presented merely as affirmations, but he is not always successful, so far as a theatre audience is concerned. The violence of Antony's fury when he sees Thidias kissing the Queen's hand shows how deeply he feels she belongs to him alone, and the whipping may be acceptable to her on that account. His offer to Caesar, shortly afterwards, telling him he may treat his freed bondsman as he likes, to 'whip, or hang, or torture', in exchange for his flogging of Caesar's emissary, is indefensible. 'Vilest things' is also troubling. Does Enobarbus mean really vile, as some sexual practices are even to a very liberal mind, or merely 'vile' as a puritan would see anything sexual without exception? It is better to understand he means the latter: that Cleopatra's allure is so overwhelming and yet so acceptable to the holy priests that they welcome it. This would be in accord with Montaigne's view, that prejudice about the genitals is unnatural,[1] though Montaigne does not go so far as Enobarbus does: 'holiness' is more like a prescient but less fervent adoption of D.H. Lawrence's praises.

John F. Danby was concerned with the 'opposites' as part of a 'peculiarly Shakespearean dialectic', when in his excellent essay on *Antony and Cleopatra*[2] he wrote 'Opposites are juxtaposed, mingled, married; then from the very union which seems to promise strength, dissolution flows'.[3] From the very outset, he convincingly argues, these opposites are first presented in the soldier's view that Cleopatra has only a gypsy's lust, that Antony is a strumpet's fool, followed by, on the contrary, Antony's protestation that his love knows no bounds, will accept no limitation whatsoever. Then follows Cleopatra's immediate taunting of Antony, her reminder to him that he is a married man, his renewed affirmation that 'the nobleness of life is to do thus [embracing], when such a mutual pair and such a twain can do't', and Cleopatra's insistence, followed by yet more toing and froing. The maids of honour Iras and Charmian then parody Cleopatra in their insatiable sexual expectations. How to choose, Danby asks, between the harsh view of the soldiers and the nobleness Antony speaks of? 'Coleridge chose the former; Dr Sitwell and Mr Wilson Knight the latter. To entertain either judgment, however, is not enough. The deliquescent truth'. Danby continues, 'is neither in them nor between them, but contains both'.[4] And again 'Antony and Cleopatra are opposed to the world that surrounds and isolates them. In this isolation their union seems absolute, infinite, and self-sufficient. Yet the war of the contraries pervades the love, too. In coming together they lapse, slide, and fall apart unceasingly.'[5]

---

[1] Montaigne, *Essais*, p.814.
[2] John F. Danby, p.XX.
[3] *Signet* (paperback) edition, p.248.
[4] *Signet,* p.252.
[5] *Signet,* p.252.

Thus far I am in agreement. It is only in his final remarks that Danby seems to me to diverge from the very position he has earlier adopted. The play, he writes,

> shows us Virtue, the root of the heroic in man, turned merely into *virtù*, the warrior's art, and both of them ensnared in the world, very force entangling itself with strength. It depicts the 'man of men' soldiering for a cynical Rome or whoring on furlough in a reckless Egypt. It is the tragedy of the destruction of man, the creative spirit, in perverse war and insensate love – the two complementary and opposed halves of a disintegrating society.[6]

This siding with only one side of the dilemma initially proposed ignores what was said about the opposites, rather than that the truth contains both – and continues to do so, as I shall now argue, up to the final curtain.

What is in Cleopatra's mind when she orders her eunuch to tell Antony she is dead? It may look like a self-centred flirtatiousness curious to see how he takes the news – she asks to be told about this – seemingly a strumpet's glorying in the expectation that he will promptly come running to her in grief, only to be reconciled when he realises she is still alive. She has acted before in this way; it is policy with her, as she tells Charmian, not to set out to please Antony – 'the way to lose him' (1.3.10) – and has tried the trick of refusing to see him when he comes pleading, in pretending to be in danger of dying, in taunting him continually. Yet at other times she convinces us as well as him that she is truly devoted. When he is putting on his armour she seems a wife desperate to help him in any way she can, showing her ignorance – to his great satisfaction, no doubt – as she tries one piece after another to fit his shoulder-piece. When, after a bout of teasing, he accuses her of 'idleness [trifling]', her reply convinces completely,

> Tis sweating labour
> To bear such idleness so near the heart
> As Cleopatra this.
> (1.3.93-5)

Yet she also speaks of herself as one of those that '*trade* in love' (2.5.1-2) and is convinced, although we are not, that, on hearing that Antony will leave to attend Fulvia's funeral, she herself will die instantly. 'I have seen her die twenty times upon far poorer moment' (1.2.143), says Enobarbus,

---

[6] *Signet* edition, p.269.

adding here a thought that may take us further into understanding what Antony and Cleopatra mean to each other: 'I think there is mettle in death, which commits some loving act upon her, she hath such a celerity in dying'. 'Dying' here has the overtones generally found in Elizabethan parlance, implying orgasm, though he has not himself witnessed any 'loving act' of hers.

This is a theme that will be taken up several times later in the play. When Cleopatra sees Iras suddenly fall dead after she has kissed her, she muses that 'The stroke of death is as a lover's pinch, Which hurts and is desired' (5.2.295-6). She herself has spoken of being 'With Phoebus amorous pinches black' (1.5.28), as though covered all over with the marks of his loving attention. Even the water in which her barge sails follows the oars faster as though 'amorous of their strokes' (2.2.203), and the suggestion here is again of something painful, rather than gentle stroking, as the oars smack down on the yielding surface.

Cleopatra's conscious intention of making Antony desire her more by continually denying him can also be interpreted in a similar sense, as truly loving. She may seem to want to master him but not in the sense of a hired dominatrix, nor is he merely humiliated as a client who prostrates himself under the whip, though the erotic effect may have some resemblance. (What should one make of the last line of 141: 'she that makes me sinne awards me paine'?)

The 'pinches' are amorous, as well as desired. Cleopatra is not concerned solely to hurt him, and her agonised begging for pardon, when she realises what humiliation her flight from the sea-battle has caused Antony is not contradicted by his insistence that 'You did know how much you were my conqueror, and that My sword, made weak by my affection, would Obey it on all cause' (3.111.65-8). She has no defence, no words but 'O, my pardon!' and again 'Pardon, pardon'. She *is* his conqueror, and has deliberately made herself so, and he has accepted that, returning to her over and over again. His reply now is entirely loving:

Fall not a tear, I say; one of them rates
All that is won and lost. Give me a kiss;
Even this repays me.
(3.12.69-71)

What would Enobarbus say to *that*? Nothing complimentary. Reckoning a kiss worth losing an empire for is either delusion or magnificent. Yet while the reconciliation convinces at the time that beneath all the domination and humiliation, there is deep love, it is still subject to what Danby calls the 'war of the contraries'.

There is a similar reversal after Antony discovers that, some years later, Cleopatra has neglected to keep her navy in good repair, so that his own fleet is conquered a second time. He is outraged as never before. 'Triple-turned whore!', 'This foul Egyptian', 'The witch shall die' (*A. and C.* 4.12.10). The Sonnets poet never goes so far as that, though he may imply such fury. Cleopatra for her part seems ignorant of the cause of his anger, as though she had no active part in destroying the fighting power of her ships. This is not a case of deliberate treachery, and her message to him that she is dead, to be worded 'piteously', is a last unplanned attempt at guile. Antony's sudden turnabout is also not a humiliated acceptance of punishment, but again loving, like the water following the oars, but with a human accent. He will 'weep for my pardon' (4.14.45) – pardon for ever having allowed an impediment, however grave, to cause his love to alter – but he is not aware that Cleopatra asked to be told how he received the news of her death. He does not have to face that impediment. The Sonnets poet and the dramatic character explain one another here. Antony resembles Desdemona in her dying moment. At the same time, there is something ironic in the scene, since we know, as he does not, that it is all for nothing, Cleopatra is far from dead. A wry comment from Enobarbus would be intolerable here, but would be merited.

Antony's next thoughts would also be rebuked by Enobarbus, if he had not already died, overcome by guilt at having abandoned Antony and by Antony's generous forgiveness, which effectively increases Antony's stature in our eyes. Suicide is not the end for Antony, as it is for Enobarbus. He imagines himself pursuing Cleopatra into the afterlife, and weeping for his pardon, as she wept for hers:

> Where souls do couch on flowers, we'll hand in hand,
> And with our sprightly port make the ghosts gaze.
> Dido and her Aeneas shall want troops,
> And all the haunt be ours.
> (4.14.51-4)

Can he mean it? Is he not aware of the unlikelihood? A little later he speaks of importuning death until he has laid his last kiss on her lips; he does not confide in her his expectation of reunion. He is unaware in fact that Cleopatra has exactly the same expectation.

Thoughts of death are inextricably interwoven here with thoughts of erotic celebration, as though their earlier relationship, the one dispensing by harshness a kind of death to the other, were continuing in a different way, as though death were in all truth their object. As he is about to fall on his sword – no mere erotic imagery or symbolism here – still supposing that Cleopatra has died, he sees her as a bride:

> I will be
> A bridegroom in my death, and run into't
> As to a lover's bed.
> (4.14.99-101)

Cleopatra, as she is robed in the majestic robes and crown of Egypt, speaks as though she had heard him:

> methinks I hear
> Antony call: I see him rouse himself
> To praise my noble act ...
> (5.2.284-6)

even imagining him kissing Iras instead of granting herself 'that kiss which is my heaven to have'. She has no reliance on his fidelity.

True lovers may die in concord, expecting future bliss. Antony and Cleopatra die separately, yet in concord too. 'I have immortal longings': longings such as women expecting childbirth have for some particular dish, but, here, longings for immortality or longings that will continue immortal after death. Cleopatra sees herself as though pregnant and giving life again: the asp she applies to her breast (not to her arm as in Plutarch) is 'my baby at my breast, That sucks the nurse asleep' – the death-dealing snake is for her nourished by the milk she remembers giving to her children. Death and life almost co-exist. Even the 'Clown' who brings the asp seems to confirm with his malapropism that 'his biting is immortal'. Carried by the words we are almost persuaded.

Iras, however, supplies what Enobarbus could not, the touch of realism: 'the bright day is done, and we are for the dark' (5.2.193-4), and Charmian's appeal to the First Guard, as she dies: 'Ah, soldier!' is for her the last utterance of her desires: she like Iras foresees no future. (Yet, 'Ah, soldier' is added to words taken from Plutarch, it is Shakespeare's hint that she, like her queen, still longs for a man.)

It remains for Caesar to pronounce the official obituary, directing that the lovers be buried together. Bland as it is, the obituary is not untrue:

> High events as these
> Strike [touch] those that make them; and their story is
> No less in pity, than his glory which
> Brought them to be lamented.
> (5.2.359-62)

Pity and glory, yes, the contraries continue. But Caesar, though he himself wept at the news of Antony's death, and rightly says

> The death of Antony
> Is not a single doom; in the name lay
> A moiety of the world.
> (5.1.17-20)

can only see the political aspect, the loss of Rome, as can Agrippa when he adds how strange it is that 'nature must compel us to lament Our most persisted deeds'. Agrippa can see how impossible it was that Antony could behave otherwise, and yet how necessary it was that he should suffer. None of the Romans is aware of what Antony meant to Cleopatra, or she to him.

The Sonnets poet makes his lover a man great beyond compare, seeing him as the sun, as Christ, as Eros, as defeating 'death and all oblivious enmity' (55.9). I argued earlier that Cleopatra's praise of Antony is to be understood in the same way, that her words to Dolabella are the words the Sonnets poet might use, if such a dialogue could take place in the confines of a sonnet-sequence.

> His legs bestrid the ocean: his reared arm
> Crested the world: his voice was propertied
> As all the tuned spheres, and that to friends;
> But when he meant to quail [make quail] and shake the orb,
> He was as rattling thunder.
> (5.2.82-86)

We never see him in the play in such a light, any more than the lover in the Sonnets actually shows such greatness. But Cleopatra will not tolerate a moment's doubt. Her conviction that they will meet beyond the grave is part of her challenge to the temporal ruler:

>   'Tis paltry to be Caesar:
> Not being Fortune, he's but Fortune's knave,
> [Lou's not Times foole. 16.9.]
> A minister of her will. And it is great
> To do that thing that ends all other deeds,
> Which shackles accidents and bolts up change;
> Which sleeps, and never palates more the dung,
> The beggar's nurse and Caesar's.
> (5.2.2-7)

Compare again the Sonnet:

> The earth can have but earth, which is his due.
> My spirit is the better part of me.
> So then thou hast but lost the dregs of life,

The pray of wormes, my body being dead.
(74.7-10)

She will still try to wriggle out of her status as a prisoner, concealing her true wealth, insincerely calling Caesar as if *he* were Antony, 'My master, and my lord!' (5.2.189) but her mind is made up. She will put on her robe and her crown, lie magnificently as the descendant of the Pharaohs (in title at least) and imagine Antony mocking Caesar, praising her noble act:

> Husband, I come:
> Now to that name my courage prove my title!
> I am fire and air, my other elements
> I give to baser life.
> (5.2.287-90)

But this is nobility mixed with supreme erotic triumph. To call Antony 'husband' sounds ordinary enough, though she sees in the title, spoken of Antony, something that takes courage to proclaim,. But 'I come' is also a confession of bodily stirrings. Hanged men are said to ejaculate. So does Cleopatra 'come' in the sense of modern and Elizabeth common parlance.[7] She announces to him both her devotion as a bride, and her moment of ecstatic union, 'dying' in both senses.

She is, Charmian says, a 'lass unparalleled' (5.2.136). She herself said earlier she was

> No more but e'en a woman, and commanded
> By such poor passion as the maid that milks
> And does the meanest chares.
> (4.15.72-4)

Though she wears such grandeur, her crown is awry, so that for an instant she is meant to look a trifle tipsy, and a moment's thought will recall that she now has no kingdom to rule. Yet the greatness of her final speeches moves to tears. No other heroine of tragedy dies with such majesty. To withhold assent and affirmation is mean. Enobarbus would not do so: his admiration for Antony extends to the queen also. The weight of the Sonnets must be added. There Shakespeare's own commitment, a commitment made in full awareness of its limitation, is clearly as intentional as Cleopatra's: he is expressing through her what he could not

---

[7] See E. Partridge, *Shakespeare's Bawdy*, 'come' – and 'husband', also the bawdy exchange on 'come' between Escalus and Pompey in *Measure for Measure*, 2.1.114-118.

realise in the short length of a poem. All the reservations about the black mistress look paltry when compared to Cleopatra. Her final moment is given amazing new life, a complement and a renewed affirmation, however much undercut by contrary indications.

Here, however, I turn to Danby's argument again, where he says that the play depicts the 'man of men' soldiering for a cynical Rome, or whoring on furlough in a reckless Egypt. 'It is', he continues, 'the tragedy of the destruction of man, the creative spirit, in perverse and insensate love – the two complementary and opposed halves of a disintegrating society'. And he is right: the lovers die for each other alone, without regard for the rest of the world. Unaware of what Octavius Caesar, the Augustus to be, intends by his 'universal peace', Antony's kiss, worth all the Roman world to him, is meaningful only to him and to Cleopatra. We the audience understand this, sympathise and even empathise with him, but we are also aware that he has brought about his own death as well as hers, that she has no thought for her children, whom Caesar has threatened to destroy if she kills herself. What Antony calls 'the nobleness of life' is noble yet not noble, grand yet small, and 'of life' can only mean the life of the lovers, not 'life' in a wider sense. Yet Brechtian 'estrangement' is not right here. Enobarbus has said enough, but he is silent now. We do not simply reproach the lovers for their perversity, they are too great for that. Our best course is to heed the Sonnets poet's words, that theirs is the lascivious grace in whom 'all il wel showes'. Allowing the opposed meanings to reflect their relationship like the gleam on shot silk, now one, now the other appearing, yet both contained in the one surface, is the way to appreciate them in terms Shakespeare would have approved. The gleam continues to oscillate for a moment in *Troilus and Cressida*, Troilus rejecting all infidelity, incapable of separating the false Cressida from the true, so closely do they come together in his mind, but finally rejecting all talk of combined opposites. He is the very reverse of Antony.

CHAPTER FIVE

A LOVER'S COMPLAINT

This poem is bound with the Sonnets in the Quarto edition (of 1609), but is not mentioned on the title-page, which refers only to the Sonnets. At the beginning of the poem itself, the attribution is, however, clear: 'By William Shake-speare'. This initial lack of attribution at one time was the source of controversy, because for many years there was a considerable volume of opinion that it was not by Shakespeare at all, Chapman's name being at one time put forward as that of the probable author. But for some fifty years, critical opinion has swung towards Shakespeare, especially since Kenneth Muir came out in favour. Demonstrations of parallel passages, recurring imagery and words used idiosyncratically in the Sonnets and plays, as well as statistical analyses, studies of grammar and syntax, have been capped by John Kerrigan's demonstration in his Penguin edition of 1986[1] (where a fuller account of scholarly research will be found) that far from being a strange appendage, *A Lover's Complaint* follows a normal practice in publishing Elizabethan poetry (see also his *Motives of Woe: Shakespeare and Female Complaint*). As Katherine Duncan-Jones has shown,[2] Daniel's *Delia* (1592) has fifty Sonnets, a short ode, and a substantial poem in rhyme royal (the rhyme-scheme also of the 'Complaint'), on the same subject as Shakespeare's poem, the seduction and abandonment of a young girl. Thomas Lodge published *Phillis* (1593) with a sonnet sequence, an ode and a long poem. In the same year Giles Fletcher the Elder's *Licia* appeared: fifty-two Sonnets followed by an ode and a dialogue, and Spenser's *Amoretti* also has a Delian structure, as has a sequence by Barnfield. The only difference is that there is no intervening ode between the Sonnets and *A Lover's Complaint*, as is usually the case in the others.

In 2007 Brian Vickers published *Shakespeare. A Lover's Complaint, and John Davies of Hereford*, arguing that John Davies – not Sir John –

---

[1] Kerrigan, pp.13-14 and 389 ff.
[2] Duncan-Jones, p.44.

was the sole author. It followed several studies by specialists concluding
that the *Complaint* is spurious, and impressed Jonathan Bate and Eric
Rasmussen so well that they omitted the poem from their *Collected Works
of Shakespeare*, published in the same year, as inauthentic.

The present chapter was complete at the time Vickers' book appeared,
and time has yet to show how well it will be received. Bate's and
Rasmussen's decision to omit the poem may become influential. However,
it is necessary to state my own position, despite the fact that I had not used
and do not now use any of Vickers' statistical methods and lexicographical
comparisons, nor can I use any of these with the expertise of Macdonald P.
Jackson (and other specialists in these fields) who have given, since
Vickers book appeared, further arguments against the authorship of Davies
and for that of Shakespeare.

It seems to me that these arguments against Davies as author are
extremely cogent, and that this must be said despite the debt owed by
scholars to Vickers' earlier work.   He had doubted Shakespeare's
authorship from the first time he read the poem, largely on the grounds that
the quality of verse was inferior, a judgment supported by several
commentators. Although Malone had written of it as a 'beautiful poem',
'in every part of which the hand of Shakespeare is visible',[3] later critics
found it stiff and awkward in style and construction. The language is
sometimes 'so full of innovation that it is difficult even to penetrate its
literal sense'.[4]

Similarly J.C. Maxwell found it hard to dissent from Mackail's verdict
of 1912 although adding: 'A certain laboriousness, a certain cramped,
gritty, discontinuous quality, affects it subtly but vitally throughout'.[5]
There are several other views like these, voiced by scholars of distinction.
Maxwell while believing the *Complaint* to be a poem of Shakespeare's
maturity, judged it 'a poem of very little merit'. He also, however, quoted
Mackail's favourable view: 'there are more than a few passages in the
poem which are like Shakespeare at his best'[6] and Kenneth Muir's: 'the
poem is inferior in most ways to Shakespeare's other narrative poems, and
it is inferior to the best of the Sonnets; but it is not without its own special
flavour ...'[7]   Kerrigan also speaks of 'aloofness, strange in diction,
contorted in syntax, inventive but sometimes opaque in imagery;   its
central human situation is at once painful and presented with an artfulness

---

[3] Quoted in Burrow, p.139.
[4] *loc.cit.*
[5] J.C. Maxwell, p.xxxiv.
[6] Maxwell, p.xxxvi.
[7] *loc.cit.*

which chills'. He also, however, speaks of it as 'This extreme, rewarding poem'.[8]

These criticisms, together with the praises accorded nevertheless, undermine Vickers. He would like to show that shortcomings in the poem imply Shakespeare could not have written it, opening the way for argument in favour of a poet of less merit, like Davies. But the instances he provides are often inappropriate. It is true that the rhyme-word 'takes', for instance, has to do duty twice over in a single stanza of the *Complaint* (ll.107-10), but the Sonnets rhyme often on one word in the same Sonnet ('thee'/'see' and 'be'/'thee' (3.9-11 and 13-14); 'usery'/'thee' and 'thee'/'posterity' (6.5-7 and 10-12); 'see'/'thee' and 'thee'/'me' (43.1.3 and 13.14), with eleven other rhymes on 'thee' in Sonnets 10 to 50. Again, Vickers notes that four rhyme-pairs occur in the poem, twice within a short space: 're-using a rhyme eleven times in a poem of 329 lines shows a paucity of invention not found in Shakespeare.'[9] In the Sonnets, however, rhymes on 'eie' are as plentiful as those on 'thee' (see 7.2-4, 9.1-3, 11.13-14, 17.5-7, 24.6-8, 46.6-8, 49.6-8, etc.).

Many other rejections, in favour of Davies, are made equally without awareness of Shakespeare's usage.[10] Shakespeare's rhymes in the plays were sometimes faulty.

In *Richard II* he rhymes 'light' with 'night' twice, and then seems reduced at the end to

> With Cain go wander through the shades of night,
> And never show thy head by day nor light.
> (*Richard II* 5.6.37-44)

but unperturbed goes on in *Pericles* (the repetition may, it is true, not this time be his) with

> She tells me here she'll wed the stranger knight,
> Or never more to view nor day, nor light.
> (*Pericles* 2.4.14-17)

Lines in the *Complaint* such as 'Oh then advance (of yours) that phraseles hand' (225) are perhaps no more clumsy than the Sonnets couplet:

---

[8] Kerrigan, p.389.
[9] Vickers, p.2.
[10] Frank Kermode has an excellent discussion of Shakespeare's poorer verse in *Timon of Athens*. See his *Shakespeare's Language*, p.231ff.

O him she stores, to show what welth she had,
In daies long since, before these last so bad.
(67.13-14)

Titus Andronicus speaks of the impossible when he says 'Give me a sword. I'll chop off my hands too' (*Titus* 3.1.72). Shakespeare himself confesses in the Sonnets that 'my gracious numbers are decayde' and speaks of his 'sick Muse' (79.3 and 4), his 'toung-tied Muse' (85.1), although it is true he also affirms that he is always guided by and dependent on his lover. Sonnet 88 is particularly touching in its willingness to accept blame, to allow the lover to 'place my merit in the eie of skorne' (88.2) and ending 'for thy right, myselfe will beare all wrong' (88.143). The poet's confidence may seem misplaced, viewed from outside, but it is the source of all his work, not merely of his 'faults conceald' (88.7).

I had always felt uncomfortable with the line in the poem 'That maidens eyes stuck over all his face' (81), and still don't admire it. But Jackson points out[11] that Timon speaks of 'the eyes and hearts of men ... That numberless upon me stuck' (4.3.261-3) and that the Duke in *Measure for Measure* exclaims 'O place and greatness! Millions of false eyes are stuck upon thee' (4.1.69-61).

The imagery from gunnery is inappropriate in

Some-times her leveld eyes their carriage ride,
As they did battry to the spheres intend:
Sometime diverted their poore balls are tide,
To th'orbed earth
(22-25)

Eyes aiming to fire at the planets are an absurd idea, but in *1 Henry VI* 4.7.79 eyes are likened to bullets to be fired at an enemy. Shakespeare often thinks of eyeballs as though they were much larger balls. Cleopatra threatens to kick the messenger's eyes as though they were footballs (*Antony and Cleopatra* 2.5.63). Bassanio asks whether the eyes in Portia's portrait are moving, or whether they are 'riding on the balls of mine' (*Merchant of Venice* 3.2.116-7) and therefore seem in motion. How could the painter have seen to do them – having made one, 'it should have power to steal both his / And leave itself unfurnished' (3.2.124-6).

The later plays especially have lapses, or involved thoughts extremely hard to understand. The verse of *Cymbeline* strikes Kermode as

---

[11] Jackson, p.20.

'overworked',[12] and the 'sheer invention of some passages' in *Coriolanus* is 'beyond the necessity of its expression'[13] For Richard Horsley the style of *Cymbeline* is 'often perverse in syntax, and sometimes so elliptical' as to raise the question whether the text is corrupt, though he prefers to think it is comparable to the 'metaphysical toughness of thought and angularity of expression' in Donne.[14]

That Shakespeare was the author of *Cymbeline* is not now questioned. There are many parallels both with the plays and the Sonnets,[15] so many that Mackail concluded that '*if* the author of *A Lover's Complaint* was not the author of the Sonnets, he had read them, or some of them, when he wrote the poem'.[16] That some of these parallels should repeat crude faults does not make them easier to read, but they do inspire some indulgence. As often happens, statistical evidence, however valuable, needs to have specific regard for the individual case.

The many parallels between the *Complaint* and the Sonnets deserve attention, since they lead towards the conclusion that the *Complaint* is a kind of palinode, in which the poet retracts or views very differently the events in the earlier part of the same volume. The girl in the poem introduces a character who is neither the lover of the Sonnets nor the black mistress, but simply one who is utterly disappointed in the love offered to her. In the Sonnets the lover is always praised by the poet, even in his misdoings, which are always presented not only in paradoxical manner but also in a good light, as are those of the mistress. The man in the poem expresses himself often in terms that would suit the lover in the Sonnets. In fact as G. Wilson Knight rightly observed, *A Lover's Complaint* 'is composed round a young man who is similar to the young man of the Sonnets' adding that the poem 'turns on what looks like a rather bitter study of the same young man';[17] several other commentators have concurred, at least in the resemblance between the Sonnets and the poem. The poem, however, is quite unparadoxical. Whereas the lover in the Sonnets is saved from criticism by the poet's fervent declarations of love, and by his defence of his faults: 'Thy adverse party is thy Advocate' (35.10), in the poem, on the contrary, the man is always under the accusing eye of the girl. He may say

---

[12] Kermode, p.264.
[13] *Ibid.*
[14] Richard Horsley in Barnet, p.1452.
[15] Jackson, p.20.
[16] *Ibid.*
[17] G. Wilson Knight, *The Mutual Flame*, pp.108 and 53

> Oh heare me tell,
> The broken bosoms that to me belong,
> Have emptied all their fountains in my well,
> And mine I powre your ocean all amonge
> (253-6)

which is echoed not only in the more tender lines addressed to the Sonnets lover

> Their images [of his loves] I view in thee,
> And thou (all they) hast all the all of me
> (31.13-14)

and even more closely in

> Thou art the grave where buried love doth live,
> Hung with the tropheis of my lovers gon,
> Who all their parts of me to thee did give.
> That due of many, now is thine alone.
> (33.9-12)

as well as in speaking of the girl as an ocean, for the Sonnets poet says similarly of the man: 'your worth (wide as the Ocean is)' (80.5). But when the man in the *Complaint* says of himself, as here, that he contains so many other loves, he seems rather to be boasting, and the poet's loving voice saying the same thing is not heard.

In the poem the man is proud of the fact that he never felt the slightest love for any of the women whom he met. In some ways he is like Bertram who rejects the love of Helena. He harmed them, but never harmed himself; he

> Kept hearts in liveries, but *mine owne was free*,
> And raignd commanding in his monarchy.
> (195-6)

In the Sonnets freedom is again prominent but regretfully, not proudly accepted:

> Farewell thou art too deare for my possessing,
> And like enough thou knowst thy estimate,
> The *Charter of thy worth gives thee releasing*:
> *My bonds in thee are all determinate.*
> (87.1-4)

A Lover's Complaint has nothing to suggest the sad recognition in the Sonnets:

> Thus have I had thee as a dream doth flatter,
> In sleepe a King, but waking no such matter.
> (87.13-14)

The man in the poem hasn't the slightest idea of what pain he has caused.

In the Sonnets the poet remembers a time when his lover was unkind, but encourages him with:

> ... your trespasse now becomes a fee,
> *Mine ransoms yours, and yours must ransom mee.*
> (120.13-14)

Each suffers for the other – at least they do so in the poet's imagination – and thereby both are saved. It is 'mutuall render onely me for thee' (125.12). For the girl in the poem, however, the reverse is true. She remembers how she yielded to the man completely, 'all melting', as he seemed also to be, whereas

> our drops this difference bore,
> His *poison'd me, and mine did him restore.*
> (300-1)

The last line here corresponds closely in form to the line about ransoms in the Sonnet, and must have been meant to be seen as the view of someone now sceptical of a lover's vows.

A different kind of parallel is the one between the words spoken by the man in the poem about a nun who was so enamoured of him that she wanted to leave her convent: *"Religious love put out religion's eye'* (250) (meaning in the first instance 'dedicated', in the second 'religious faith'). This is said as a demonstration of male prowess. In the Sonnets the poet writes:

> How many a holy and obsequious teare
> *Hath deare religious love stolne from mine eye,*
> (31.5-6)

meaning that his belief, inspired by religion, led him to weep at the loss of his lovers, whereas he now realises they are all part of the man he adores:

> Their images I lov'd, I view in thee,
> And thou (all they) hast all the all of me.
> (31.13-14)

What the Sonnets poet sees as comfort, the man in the poem sees as a
means of flattery: 'How mightie then you are' (251) – he who could attract
a nun so strongly is himself, he declares, overpowered by the girl. It is true
that he then goes on to say *'For thou art all and all things els are thine'*
(266), echoing *'thou (all they) hast all the all of me'*, just quoted. But this
too sounds very different from the loving tone of the Sonnets poet. The
poet, after all, adored his lover as *'my sun'* (33.9). The man in the poem is
merely proud of this: 'My parts had powre to charm *a sacred Sunne'*
(260).

In the Sonnets the affirmation 'I am that I am' (121.9), and the refusal
to allow others to judge the poet by their own standards is questionable,
but saved from mere egotism by the poet's assurance that he can dispense
with criticism because he is so identified with a lover who is in some sense
divine, however ambiguously (112.9-14). It is this assurance that leads the
poet into such lapses as I have indicated, though occasionally also into the
glorious moments of poetry found in both plays and Sonnets. Swinburne
singled out the lines

> O father, what a hell of witchcraft lies
> In the small orb of one particular tear!
> (ll.288-9)

In the poem there is again a contrast, when the man says

> All my offences that abroad you see
> Are errors of the blood, none of the mind.
> (183-84)

going on to declare that 'Love made them not', and that the women who
fell in love with him 'sought their shame':

> And so much lesse of shame in me remaines,
> By how much of me their reproch containes,
> (188-89)

He has done harm to them, he admits, but 'nere was harmed' (194). Others
hearts were kept in liveries, but his own was free, and in proof of his
devotion to the girl who now complains he gives her all the gems, jewels,
Sonnets, given to him by all the others. These are the *'trophies'*, as he
calls them (218), recalling the *trophies* in Sonnet 31.10, which are not
treated with such lack of love for the donors, and these are the rings and
letters which the girl throws into the river at the start of the poem. No such
dismissal greets any protestation of love offered in the Sonnets.

Yet the argument still remains, in the parallel situation in both poem and Sonnets, whereby the lover seems to love in a quasi-religious sense. We have seen earlier how the poet in the Sonnets article compares his lover to the sun, to a 'God in love', a love 'buylded far from accident' (124.5). In *A Lover's Complaint* the man tells the girl he must give up the love-tokens 'where I myselfe must *render*' (219) (compare nature's 'Quietus', which is 'to *render* thee' (126.12)). She is his 'origin and ender', his Alpha and Omega, and therefore:

> these of force must your *oblations* be,
> Since I their Aulter, you enpatrone me.

In the Sonnets, the poet begged the lover 'take thou my *oblacion* poore but free' (125.10). 'Oblation' has in both instances a religious implication, the wafer of the Eucharist. But in *A Lover's Complaint*, although the man is giving up his love-tokens, they must include the woman's offering. He is the altar, and only gives in order to receive back. She makes him thus her patron. The sense may be like that of the well-known hymn: 'New treasures still of countless price, God does provide for sacrifice': God gives only to claim again: '*do ut des*'. But all this is of no effect. The tokens end up not on an altar but in the river.

The river recalls 'how deceits were *guilded* in his smiling' (172), alluding to the alchemical transmutation that in Sonnet 33 '*guilded* pale streams', and even momentarily transformed the Sonnets poet himself. Antony, in Cleopatra's eyes, was like the Philosophers' Stone, passing his own greatness to others, gilding them. In *A Lover's Complaint* the transmutation is dismissed as mere deceit.

In the Sonnets the lover is both man and god (Sonnet 34). In the poem the man is enchanting,

> For on his visage was in little drawne,
> What largenesse thinks in parradise was sawn.
> (90-1)

The strange final line is intended to mean that the man's face was a microcosm reflecting the paradisal macrocosm. Perhaps the desire to indicate that this was not really so induced Shakespeare to present the thought in such a deformed shape.

There are several suggestions in the Sonnets that the lover is a man of feminine appearance, and symbolically a combination of male and female representing in alchemy and neo-Platonist tradition a divinity. In *A Lover's Complaint* occurs a similar passage to this same purpose:

His qualities were beauteous as his forme,
For *maiden* tongu'd he was and thereof free;
Yet if men mov'd him, was he such a storme
As oft twixt May and April is to see
(99-103)

The feminine grace of his voice and the rough manly passion of his anger point in the same direction as the Sonnets.

The most interesting evidence that *A Lover's Complaint* is by Shakespeare is found in the description of the man by the girl. It has been interpreted in various ways, and my own interpretation must rely in part on what I have said earlier about the ways in which Shakespeare in the Sonnets alludes to his own name. The stanza is certainly not intended to make any frank avowal, yet many descriptions point in the same direction:

So on the tip of his subduing tongue
All kinde of arguments and questions deepe,
Al *replication prompt*, and reason strong
For his advantage still did wake and sleep,
To make *the weeper laugh, the laugher weepe*
He *had the dialect and different* skil,
Catching al passions in his craft of will.
(120-126)

The immediately preceding lines have spoken of the man's management of horses. In the stanza quoted, however, it is his linguistic prowess that is praised, his 'subduing [conquering] tongue'. He engaged in 'all kinds of arguments and questions deep': that is, as Colin Burrow interprets, in 'persuasive proofs and profound debates', although also in 'replication prompt', or 'quick replies', perhaps repartee, adds Katherine Duncan-Jones. This leads Burrow to see a rhetorician here, although that seems less appropriate when the man is said to 'make the weeper laugh, the laugher weepe'. That he 'had the dialect' means he had 'an "effective" manner of speaking' (Duncan-Jones) or 'had a verbal knack' (Kerrigan) or 'could catch different idioms and different modes of speech' (Burrow). 'Catching all passions' is for Kerrigan: '(1) snaring everyone's feelings, capturing the affection of all who heard him; (2) enmeshing in his speech every kind of strongly moving emotion', and for Burrow (a) capturing each human emotion in a skilful display of artistry; (b) winning over everyone's emotions in a crafty display of control'. All these descriptions fit, even better than a lawyer or rhetorician, a dramatist or actor.

The next stanza reads:

That he didde in his general bosome raigne
Of young, of old, and sexes both inchanted,
To dwel with him in thoughts, or to remaine
In personal duty, following where he haunted,
Consent's bewitcht, ere he desire have granted,
And dialogu'd for him what he would say,
Askt their own wils and made their wils obey.
(127-133)

His reign in the general bosom suggests the Sonnets as in 'Thy bosome is indeared with all hearts' (Duncan-Jones), although the sense here is rather 'the affections of everyone' (Burrow). Young, old, and 'sexes both' were enchanted, and dwelled with him in thoughts, or followed him to the place where he 'habitually resorted' (Duncan-Jones). 'The loving consent (of those who encountered him) was won by enchantment, before he had even acknowledged his desires' (Duncan-Jones). 'And dialogu'd for him what he would say' (132): 'invented dialogue for him to say what he wanted' (Kerrigan) or 'have spoken his side of the conversation on his behalf' (Burrow) or – best of all for my interpretation – 'expressed in dialogue form' what he would say (Duncan-Jones). That they 'askt their own wils and made their wils obey' (133) is not commented on by any of the three editors I have been quoting, but may be understood to mean that these people of very various conditions and natures made themselves admirers. This line, and the phrase 'in personal duty' – as servants – are the only features that do not definitely suggest the relationship of an actor or dramatist to his audiences. The discussion of serious matters is one in which the dramatist is involved. Quick answers may be repartees. The ability to produce tears or laughter certainly belongs to both actors and dramatists, as does the effective manner of speaking, the use of idioms and different modes of speech, and the emotions in them. Universal popularity is what all men and women in the theatre look for, and so is loving consent in the audience. It is true that the audience does not produce dialogue for the author, but the characters he invents can often develop a side of their personality he did not expect, and so tell him what to say. The stanzas about the man's horsemanship is irrelevant to the dramatist or actor, but the author of the poem needs to mask his meaning a little, as he may do also with the mention of a personal duty. But there is only a little masking in the expression 'craft of will'. That this craft 'catches all passions' suits a dramatist very well. That it is the craft of the playwright 'Will' is the revelation that peeps through, clearly not meant to be perfectly obvious, although the several uses of 'Will' in the Sonnets help to establish the point more solidly. There is much to connect Shakespeare himself with the lover and the poet in the Sonnets:

Be of thy selfe so wary
As I not for my selfe, but for thee will
(22.9-10)

with its double sense and pun on the name, and

So true a foole is love, that in your Will,
(Though you doe any thing) he thinks no ill.
(57.13-14)

and the many repetitions of 'Will' in 135 and 136, ending 'for my name is
Will', are among the passages where the poet affirms that he is
Shakespeare and that he shares an identity with the man he loves.

It has often been thought that he was alluding to his life as an actor
when he said he had 'made my selfe a motley to the view' (110.2),
although recent commentators prefer to associate 'motley' with the
costume of a theatrical Fool, rather than a dramatist. The lament that the
poet has been obliged to earn a living by 'publick meanes which publick
manners breeds' (111.4) suggests to Kerrigan that this was 'by means of
acting and presenting composed plays' and to Duncan-Jones by public
money, such as that paid by those who attend 'public' theatres; she relates
it to John Davies of Hereford's comment on Shakespeare's having
jeopardized his social position by his career as an actor. The succeeding
lines:

And almost thence my nature is subdu'd
To what it workes in, like the Dyers hand.
(111.6-7)

are interpreted by Kerrigan as distantly suggesting the poet's hand,
steeping language in rhetorical 'colours'. None of these comments imply
definite association with Shakespeare, whether a dramatist, poet, or actor.
The same is true of 'craft of will'. One may add, however, that if the
poet's 'nature' is 'subdued' to the characters of a play on which he is
working, it may very well have led him to fear being taken over
completely. This is the fear of the poet when he writes of an actor who is
terrified by 'some fierce thing repleat with too much rage, whose strengths
abundance weakens his owne heart' (23.3-4). To see one's hand dyed,
exactly as Lady Macbeth sees hers, could have produced an almost
overwhelming sense of irredeemable guilt.

In *A Lover's Complaint* Shakespeare has taken on the rôle of a woman
rather like Ophelia, who has been rejected by a man in some ways
reminiscent of Hamlet. In the play he had written a part for a man who
loves Hamlet, his 'sweet prince', with a dedication like that of the Sonnets

poet. To reverse this now, and see the Prince only as a possible parallel to a selfish unloving despiser must have presented some difficulties. Removing the stain from the dyer's hand was well-nigh impossible, but he launches into a palinode that allows no defence. This means abandoning the saving grace of the approval of the young man, who is lost in the person of this new so-called lover, and can no longer restore the poet's confidence in his own love or his ability to write. Here we have perhaps an expression of why some lines in the *Complaint* are so poor in quality. In the Sonnets there was always a possibility of a loophole. He may have almost despaired:

O blame me not if I no more can write
(103.5)

My tonge-tide Muse in manners holds her still
(85.1)

Where art thou Muse that thou forgetst so long ...
(100.1)

O truant Muse ...
(101.1)

        some time I hold my tongue:
Because I would not dull you with my songe
(102.13-14)

But he was always able to regain his confidence. So long as his lover approved all was well:

In so profound *Abisme* I throw all care
Of others voices, that my Adders Sence,
To critick and to flatterer stopped are
(112.9-11)

His love is 'so strongly in my purpose bred
That all the world besides me thinks y'are dead'
(112.13-14)

Because his love was so strong, he could provide himself with these paradoxical strengths. But in the *Complaint* he has no such support. The man in the poem is seen by a girl who has no use for these paradoxes, so that the Sonnets poet, in so far as he identifies with her, has no resources left: if he blunders, and he does so in the *Complaint* more frequently than anywhere else, he has no means of combating his 'adder's (deaf) sense'.

Lines that he could not allow, which he merely mentions in the Sonnets as possibilities, the weak moments of his Muse, now stand uncorrected, undismissed. Committed to this 'opposite' of the Sonnets, he can only go on with his deliberate contrast. Losing the lover's support he may have tried to persuade himself that the paradox still held, that the 'ill' still showed 'well', even though it showed up all too well.

The *Complaint* is thus a reverse or opposite of the Sonnets, rather as Pyramus and Thisbe parallels the final scene in *Romeo and Juliet*, and as Bottom's vision parallels the vision in Sonnet 33, as Touchstone's marriage to the 'foul' Audrey does the Sonnets poet's love for the 'black' or, as she is sometimes called, the 'foul' mistress, the opposite in the play to the marriage of Orlando and Rosalind. Will is both the adoring lover of the Sonnets and the egotist of the *Complaint*. And yet Will Shakespeare is also more than either. Similarly the universal vision of Diotima, apparently, though not really, without any sexual or erotic taint, is opposite to the seemingly universal erotic receptivity of the 'Will' in Sonnets 135 and 136, and the triumphant self-assertion of 'I am that I am' (121.9) in opposition to the devastating self-abasement of many other Sonnets.

A kind of paradox still remains at the end of both the *Complaint* and the last two Sonnets, that curious pair with almost identical content, quite different in tone from the rest of the Sonnets. In these, although he has just accused himself of perjury for calling the mistress kind, loving, constant and true, he still asserts his thraldom to her ending in triumph:

Love's fire heates water, water cooles not love
(154.14)

The woman in the *Complaint* ends on a similar note. The 'infected moisture' in the man's eye, the 'false fire' in his cheek, the 'forc'd thunder' from his heart are still, she fears, capable of betraying her and of perverting anew 'a reconciled Maide' (326). In both poems the poet is unable to escape from the whirling dance of opposites, but leaves them at a point where they both in their contrasting ways reaffirm love. So far as I can see that is the one stable concern in both the Sonnets and the *Complaint*, and it is part of what he means by 'I AM'.

CHAPTER SIX

THE MUSE

Hugo von Hofmannsthal compares the writing of poetry to a spider that throws its thread ahead of it in a line through the air which it then climbs along or draws into itself wherever the wind takes it. The web seems to come from nowhere. It has no purpose, as a thread, but as it becomes involved in the spider's life it takes on meaning. Poetry, or for that matter any creative writing, including even some academic writing and some journalism, is similar, but purposefulness increases as writing begins to have more of a practical, realistic aim. Words appear on the page that have never been thought of, or only vestigially; they join up and form wholes, and in poetry they may have unexpected beauty, though this may need some refining before it becomes acceptable. There is a mystery about this – how did I come to say that? Is it any good?, but also 'How do I know what I think till I see what I say?' The main idea is that poetry comes into the world without any apparent reason: 'provokes itself', and then, like the spider's web in Hofmannsthal's lines, pursues a path that it has itself created.

If the poet's inspiration is from without, it may seem, as W.B. Yeats wrote, that the poet 'becomes, as all mystics have believed, a vessel of the creative power of God'.[1] Keats said that some thoughts or expressions 'struck him with astonishment and seemed rather the production of another person than his own.[2] George Sand spoke of an emotion that 'comes, but I can find nothing in my self. It is *the other* who sings as he likes, well or ill, and when I try to think about it, I am afraid and tell myself that I am nothing, nothing at all'.[3] Dickens spoke of a 'beneficent power' that

---

[1] Yeats, 'The Return of Ulysses' in *Essays*, London, 1924, pp.248-9, quoted in Rosamond E.M. Harding, *An Anatomy of Inspiration*, Cambridge (Heffer), p.66.

[2] Harding, p.14, quoting A. Lowell, *John Keats*, 2 vols, London: Jonathan Cape, 1924, I. 501-2.

[3] Harding, p.14, quoting A.L. McKenzie, *The George Sand – Gustave Flaubert Letters*, London: Duckworth, 1922, pp.32-3.

showed all of his book to him.[4] For Shakespeare, with thoughts of Plato's universal vision of love and of Hamlet's kingdom of infinite space in mind, such inspiration could appear to confirm his belief in them. Yet the inspiration also seemed to come from within, from his own self, from the lover and from the beloved.

A surprising number of Sonnets are about the poet's indebtedness to his Muse, treating two themes, the decay of the poet's verse and the superior quality of some by a rival or rivals. Who these were is as much a mystery as the identity of the lover. Even the Muse is not easily understood: at the start of the Rival Poet cluster the lover seems to be intended: 'So oft have I invok'd thee for my Muse' (78.1) clearly says the lover has inspired the poet. But we think of the lover as masculine in this part of the collection, and Muses are always feminine in Greek myth, as the poet realises when he adds 'I grant thou wert not married to my Muse' (82.1), acknowledging that the lover is indeed male, granting so much incongruity, but continuing to write about him as the ideal source of poetry, as though he were the female Muse nevertheless. This is the better understood if we recall the hermaphrodite figure of 20 and the comparison with both Adonis and Helen in 53.

But the poet is not alone in being inspired by the Muse. Others are just as indebted as he is:

Every *alien* pen hath got my use
And under thee their poesie disperse
(78.3-4)

although, the poet adds, it is he himself who profits most by his Muse's influence: 'in others workes thou doost but mend the stile' (78.11).

We may understand here that the great beauty and grace of the lover are admired by other poets also. But that is not the same as being their Muse: again there is a double sense, one referring to the mortal man, the other to the immortal Muse in him. There is further sexual sense in 'pen' and 'use', which in several Sonnets means sexual intercourse ('I cannot blame thee, for my love thou usest', 40.6), while 'pen', as Partridge observes in *Shakespeare's Bawdy*, is used punningly when Gratiano says he will 'mar the young clerk's pen' (*The Merchant of Venice* 5.1.237). This leads to extraordinary ambiguity when the poet addresses the Muse:

---

[4] Harding, p.15, quoting T.W.T. Ley, London: Cecil Palmer, 1928, p.720.

Sing to the eare that doth thy laies esteeme,
And gives thy pen both skill and argument.
(100.7-8)

for 'thy pen' is the pen in the poet's hand, and yet the Muse's pen at the same time. There is no distinction between them.

We now hear that the poet has had to yield to other poets, to the detriment of his own verse. When he alone called for help, his poetry had all the grace of the lover, but now his 'sick muse' has yielded to another. It sounded at first as though the lover were still the Muse, not merely the beauty made known through the Muse, but now, without warning, the Muse, sick, is some other being. Yet again there is ambiguity in the poet. He grants that his lover deserved a worthier pen,

Yet what of thee thy Poet doth invent,
He robs thee of, and payes it thee againe.
(97.7-8)

Who is 'thy Poet'? He seems at first to be the rival, temporarily 'thy' poet. Yet as the Sonnet continues it seems to be about the Sonnets-poet himself, who has no power to say anything but what the Muse or the lover inspires in him.

The rival poets become one poet in 80, and the Sonnets-poet begins to falter, as the others' verse takes on the dimensions of a great galleon, while he is merely a 'sawcie barke' (80.7), like one of Drake's ships challenging the Armada.

In 86 the poet is almost overcome by the prowess of his rival – but now the rival is inspired not by the Muse, but perhaps by some spirit 'taught by spirits to write' (86.5), as though by witches. Yet no, he persuades himself, it was not fear of any such ghost that made him silent. What struck him dead was 'when your countenance fild up his line' (86.13): the beauty of the lover's face was now the whole subject of the rival's verse, and thus aroused fear that the Muse was no longer needed, essentially, for the creation of the lover's beauty. Anyone could write of it equally well.

For a while the rival-poet sequence ends on this note. The Sonnets-poet resumes with bantering surprise at the Muse's long silence – was she inspiring someone else? in which case, let her take another look at his lover – not now identical with her – and if any wrinkles have appeared in his cheeks let her satirize Time as the supposed victor over beauty. Again in 101 he chides the Muse in a very confidential way: 'Oh truant Muse what shall be thy amends' (101.1) and 'make answere Muse' (101.5). He offers her a few suitable excuses, and finally, in a complete reversal of roles, takes over from her:

Then do thy office, Muse, I teach thee how,
To make him seeme long hence, as he showes now.
(101.13-14)

Hitherto everything has depended on the Muse's inspiration. The poet
now shoulders the whole responsibility, while she is told to just get on with
the job she is supposed to be so good at, inspired by him. The mystery of
inspiration comes full circle here. Like Hofmannsthal's spider's web, the
inspiration comes from the poet, and yet seems to be from somewhere
beyond him. The great beauty of the lover too, like Antony's greatness in
Cleopatra's imagination, is imagined by the poet, and yet to restrict it to
this source is, in the words Cleopatra uses to put down Dolabella, to 'lie,
up to the hearing of the gods'.

In 103 the Muse is still inspiring poor stuff: 'Alack what poverty my
Muse brings forth' and the poet seems to discard her completely,
addressing the rest of the Sonnet to the lover. 'Blame me not', he begs, 'if
I no more can write' (103.5). Rather, the lover should look into a mirror
and see that the face there is greater than anything the poet could ever
invent. (As Cleopatra's vision is superior even to her imagined Antony.)
Why should the poet try to improve on it? Leaving the Muse completely
to one side, the poet urges the lover to be content with the mirror-image of
his beauty.

And more, much more then in my verse can sit,
Your owne glasse shows you, when you looke in it.
(103.13-14)

This counsel of despair allows no scope for the poet at all. But the
cause of all these new paradoxes is the sense that Shakespeare himself
must have had, that the stream of wonderful poetry he could sometimes
produce was his alone, and yet not his, inspired by some other being that
was all the same not independent of him. To call inspiration a Muse is
rather like a prophet saying that his prophecy is spoken to his ear by God,
or a Delphic oracle claiming to have direct knowledge of a mysterious
underworld, when more sceptical clients suspect she is inventing
ambiguous words that can be taken as the client thinks best suits him. In
all these inspirations there is an implied belief that the Muse or the God or
the underworld exists 'out there'. By naming it, it acquires reality, but it
has no more reality than the words themselves. To say 'the Muse told me
…' is not to create any real being with a reality like that of a human being.
As twentieth century theologians like John Robinson have maintained, God
can only be the knowledge of him in any human consciousness: nobody
has the right to say his own knowledge corresponds to a confirming reality

outside himself, and the same holds for a Muse. Yet both the prophet and the poet astonish themselves and everyone else with the incomparable quality of their language. Isaiah feels this as much as Shakespeare: he tells us his lips were touched with burning coal, as though to assure him that the words he wrote down did not come from his own lips. But Shakespeare, without using any such symbolism, inquires more about the meaning and the validity of his utterance. Ben Jonson may have told him, in a remark now well known, that while he 'never blotted out a line', he would have done better to blot a thousand, though Jonson added at once that he loved the man this side idolatry. There are passages in the plays, and a few in the Sonnets too, that would fit well into an anthology of bad verse such as Wyndham Lewis's 'Stuffed Owl'. The idea that inspiration comes in perfection, without need for any intervention by the poet, is a fallacy. Keats worked over and over his drafts for the Ode to Autumn, not noticing after many repetitions that he was still writing 'while wam slumpers creep', and yet creating that masterpiece.[5] Beethoven began to hear a jingle that interested him, and developed it countless times until it emerged finally as the music for the first words of 'Freude, schöner Götterfunken' in the Choral Symphony. Shakespeare seems not to have worked like that. There are some variations between the early versions of Sonnets published separately long before the others, but his way of seeing his writing was rather to accept whatever came his way. We have seen what momentary disasters that could allow, in some of the word-play in the Sonnets. It was all part of his 'submission' to the lover who was in some way himself, so that

> In so profound *Abisme* I throw all care
> Of others voices, that my Adders sence,
> To cryttick and to flatterer stopped are
> (112.9-10)

(adders are supposed to be deaf) and

> You are so strongly in my purpose bred,
> That all the world besides me thinkes y'are dead.
> (112.13-14)

There is no need to emend the last line here. His meaning is that he and his lover (himself) are so closely knit that the lover seems no longer to exist, and even the poet thinks so too. There is confirmation for him here,

---

[5] M. Ridley, p.286.

momentarily, that his absolute claims are justified. He still identifies himself with some cosmic power even as he remains an individual, with all the faults an individual can have.

CHAPTER SEVEN

VARIED PERCEPTIONS OF PHILOSOPHIES OF OPPOSITES

There have been European philosophers who saw the world in terms of opposites for two thousand five hundred years, although almost from the outset Aristotle strongly opposed: 'It is clearly hopeless to argue with a man who says nothing definite, answering neither 'yes' nor 'no', but only 'yes and no'.[1] The best known philosopher of that time today is Heraclitus, quoted in the epigraph of T.S. Eliot's *Four Quartets* for his paradox: 'The path up and the path down is one and the same'.[2] This is not remotely like the course of the Wheel of Fortune, in which Richard II sees himself sink as his rival Bolingbroke rises (*R2* 3.3). The paradoxes of the Sonnets, however, though we may trace them to this source or that, are part of a genetic inheritance with many different contributors, not all of whom are concerned with love.

Far distant in space from this kind of thinking, and yet in some ways close is the system of Taoism, which may owe its existence to some kind of communication between East and West along the ancient Silk Road. The diagram of the Tao, popular today, is a circle divided by a sinuous line that forms two comma-like shapes, the wider part of one embracing, as it were the narrower part or tail of the other. One is dark, the other light, and they are known as the Yin and the Yang, the male and female principles. However, each half, the dark one and the light, contains in itself a complete circle divided in just the same way as the initial circle is, and each of these much smaller halves contains yet another circle of the same kind, and so on *ad infinitum*, as in a set of Chinese mirrors.

A simple meaning of Tao is shown in a small sculpture in the Gulbenkian Museum, Durham, showing a man and woman revelling in sexual intercourse. But however profound the infinite ramifications are, there is no connection with the apparently similar thought of Heraclitus.

---

[1] Aristotle, p.13
[2] G.S. Kirk and J.E. Raven, p.189.

Belief and unbelief may be contraries but they are not related to the sex of the believer and the unbeliever.

Taoism remains attractive all the same, partly because it is arcane, partly because the opposites are so apparently inclusive, and yet admittedly not so. I quote an ingenious limerick not in derision, in view of the wide acceptance of such ideas, but as saying succinctly what is often implied throughout the whole history of the tradition:

> Said an erudite sinologue, How
> Shall I try to exemplify Tao?
>   It is Yes; it is No,
>   It is Stop; it is Go.
> But it's neither. D'you understand now?[3]

'It's neither'. Rejecting its very basis, Tao creates a fundamental opposition: it is the all-embracing system it claims to be, and yet is not – and this meant not in a mood of humble awareness of the human condition, but as an inherent example of the system it denies. There are often similar rejections in Shakespeare.

Two of the most influential Renaissance philosophers, Baldassare Castiglione and Nicholas of Cusa, again differed from one another in their presentation of the opposites. For Castiglione goodness necessitates evil: 'there would be no justice in the world if there were no wrongs, no magnanimity if none were pusillanimous, no continence if there were no incontinence'.[4] This questionable view – justice must define injustice, but does not thereby create it, and a magnanimous man may have no conception of small-mindedness – differs from Cusanus's treatment of the opposites, since for Cusanus they exist only in the experience of mortal men. In God only they are combined. Shakespeare, however, sees his lover as combining opposites in a godlike way, even as he sees him as at the same time an ordinary human being.

Out of all the throng of neo-Platonists and alchemists of Shakespeare's time, Paracelsus was one of the best known, and out of the huge array of ideas he put forward in his brilliant career, it may be, as Grudin argues, that of the evil hidden in the good influenced Shakespeare. Certainly Friar Lawrence's speech on the poison held within a flower (*R. and J.* 2.3.23-4) is consonant with this idea, also found in alchemy, where it is often said that the essential ingredient for creating the Stone is a poison. For those

---

[3] I do not know the name of the author.
[4] Castiglione, *Il Cortegiano* 2.2. transl. Singleton, p.92, quoted by Grudin, *Mighty Opposites*, p.20. I don't accept Grudin's argument generally, as applied to Shakespeare.

who took the symbolical meaning, this meant 'death to self'. Others may have understood literally, and paid the price. But even so, Friar Lawrence's poison has no such beneficent effect. Romeo's last words are in one sense paradoxical: 'Thus with a kiss I die' – he dies not in sexual ecstasy, as in the accepted Elizabethan ambiguity, but in real earnest, and there is no beyond, no union beyond the grave. The poison he uses is not Friar Lawrence's, but a deadly and unambiguous one, bought in Mantua of the apothecary. Grudin's argument in favour of a Paracelsian influence here does not convince.

Jacob Boehme's influence spread across Germany for two centuries after his death in 1624, and from there to the United States. Pietists of the kind who influenced Schleiermacher were deeply indebted to him, and as I have said, he wrote entirely in terms of symbolical alchemy, without a hint of real furnaces, retorts, grimy pots and pans. Hegel, whose influence in nineteenth-century Germany was great, acknowledged his indebtedness to him as the basis of his thinking.[5] What emerged from the unexpected connection was Hegel's huge system embracing history, the history of literature, aesthetics, the role of world-leaders, mostly in terms of opposites and the synthesis of opposites – Boehme's Sulphur and Mercury in a new guise. Hegel impressed his many disciples further with the apparent similarity of his argument with Christian ideas of the Holy Trinity: the Spirit was making its presence known cumulative by these progressive combinations and disruptions and renewed combinations. I restrict myself here, however, to considering what might have happened if Shakespeare had been inclined to write *Measure for Measure* in terms of Hegel's analysis of Sophocles *Antigone*, which reflects some of the principal features of his thought.

The *Antigone* is the story of a woman who insists on burying her brother Polyneices who has fallen in battle in an attack on Thebes. Doing so, she comes into conflict with Creon, the ruler of Thebes, who forbids any show of sisterly feeling for an enemy. Since Antigone insists, he condemns her to be immured until she dies of starvation. This 'absolute example of tragedy' is interpreted by Hegel in terms of a philosophy of opposites: 'Creon is not in the wrong; he maintains that the law of the State, the authority of the government is to be held in respect, and that punishment follows the infraction of the law'. Antigone, however, also, as the representative of family love, of what is holy and what belongs to the inner life, necessarily comes into collision with the State. But each of the two sides realises one of these moral powers, and has only one of these as its content; this is the element of one-sidedness here, and the meaning of

---

[5] Taylor, p.520.

eternal justice is shown in this, that both end in injustice just because they
are one-sided, though at the same time they obtain justice too. Both are
recognised as having a value of their own with untroubled course of
morality … It is only the one-sidedness in their claims which justice comes
forward to oppose.'[6]

That version of Sophocles' play can be rejected on the ground that it
takes no account of the condemnation of Creon not only by the wise
Tiresias, but by the suicide of his son and wife. If we consider, however,
how Shakespeare might have written in a similar situation, it is to *Measure
to Measure* that we turn, seeing Isabella in comparison with Antigone, and
Angelo in comparison with Creon. Isabella, like Antigone, is certainly in a
dilemma: she is right, as a nun about to enter her novitiate, to refuse to lie
with Angelo, but wrong to reject her brother's plea that she should
sacrifice her virginity, in so far as she does so with such harsh contempt.
Love is much more clearly an issue here than in the *Antigone*. But one
does not think of her at the time as an example of duality-in-unity; rather
one experiences with her the painful impossibility of satisfying either one
or the other demand made on her. Angelo, on the other hand, is simply
wrong, however much one may sympathise with him in his position of
power, able to satisfy his desires if he wishes, 'because he can'. The play
as a whole is not about any polarities that are reconcilable in eternal
justice, to use Hegel's phrase. It is about a ruler who is forced by
subterfuge to admit he has acted unpardonably, but is pardoned all the
same. The framework is Christian in a well-established tradition. If
Shakespeare has anything anywhere to say about cosmic questions is in the
mention of the 'world-soul, dreaming on things to come; (107.2), with who
knows what fearful destiny in mind for human beings.

Beginning with Kant and his antinomies, in which he undertook, to the
dismay of Aristoteleans, by purely logical means to demonstrate that the
world both must have had a beginning in time, and could not have done so,
and several other contradictions of a similar kind, the great German
philosophers of the nineteenth century all wove their systems around a
series of dialectical contrasts. Marx famously inverted Hegel, interpreting
the dialectic not as a progression of the Spirit but one of material
circumstances, ending with a society in which all shared in equal
ownership, combining individual and society in one.

Bertolt Brecht, a Marxist, made clear use of the dialectic in the titles of
two short plays, *He who Said Yes*, and *He who Said No*. His well-known
'estrangement theory' (*Verfremdung*) presents the contrast more subtly,
presenting on stage a reality from which the audience is expected to

[6] Paolucci, p.325.

dissent, and to be led towards a Marxist critique of society in general. Shakespeare presents contrasting views in the *Sonnets*, but does not seek to influence the audience by 'estrangement' in the plays.

Heinrich von Kleist's plays and stories, based on a misunderstanding of Kant, are constructed to convey paradoxes. The rebel who is denied justice and burns down cities is 'the most upright and the most horrendous' man of his time. The general who disobeys orders is promoted commander-in-chief. The play *Penthesilea* shows the Amazon queen of that name, besieging Troy, in love with Achilles, but believing he despises her, challenging him to a duel. He, in love with her, comes to the duel with neither shield nor weapon; she, in a rage, hurls herself at him, urging on wild animals who rip him to pieces. As she sinks, dying with remorse, she says there is no distinction between kissing and biting. One of her maidens pronounces her epitaph: 'And yet 'twas love that crowned him'.

Antony is defenceless against Cleopatra's cruel message that she is dead, and she herself speaks of lovers' kisses that are bites, but Shakespeare remains within the bounds of probability. Kleist was, however, aiming at a truth which Goethe – who regarded him with disfavour, stated in a much wider context. His Faust reflects that when we reach some great summit of spiritual striving, and the gates of insight are wide open, a sea of flames bursts out, so that we are unable to say whether they are flames of love or of hatred: 'Ist's Lieb, ist's Hasz, die glühend uns umwinden?'[7] Faust, unable to bear the vision, turns his back on the sun, remaining content with contemplation of the rainbow, created by the sun's flames. But Goethe did not renounce in the same way, and we shall see a similar paradox in T.S. Eliot.

Shakespeare's Utopia, or rather Gonzalo's, ridiculed at every moment by Sebastian and Alonso, begins 'I'th' commonwealth I would by contraries Execute all things' (T 2.1.152), although he does not mean by 'contraries' any reference to dialectics, merely 'contrary to normal ways of thinking and behaviour. It is an anarchist society, resembling more the Marxist idea that after the dictatorship of the proletariat the State would wither away. The society, to call it by that name, would thus correspond to a world in which differences had ceased – in one sense resembling a final stage in a dialectical process:

> For no kind of traffic [trade]
> Would I admit; no name of magistrate;
> Letters should not be known; riches, poverty
> And use of service, none; contract, succession,
> Bourn, bound of land, tilth, vineyard, none;

---

[7] *Faust Part 2*, First Act.

No use of metal, corn, or wine, or oil;
No occupation; all men idle, all;
And women too, but innocent and pure;
No sovereignty.
(*I* 2.1.152-161)

There would be no treason, felony or sword, pike, knife or gun, but nature would bring forth 'all foison, all abundance to feed my innocent people'.

It is of course not an ideal of Gonzalo's only, but a word for word translation, apart from the mention of women, of Montaigne's ideas in 'Des Cannibales' about the Indians of the newly-discovered Americas, those vast plains which seemed to offer infinite riches without hindrance to those Europeans prepared to exploit them.

Schopenhauer's masterpiece, *The World as Will and Imagination [Vorstellung]* again touches on a Shakespearean theme without appearing to do so intentionally. This is partly because his concept of 'Will' [Wille]; resembles, without intending to, Shakespeare's use of his own name, especially in Sonnets 135 and 136. As in the Sonnets, 'Will' in Schopenhauer is both the individual Will, and the great Will in all creation. It manifests itself in reality rather as Hegel's Spirit did, but with far different manifestations. Thus it is hunger, and manifests itself in teeth; it is sexual appetite, and manifests itself in the phallus; in everything that exists the Will is present as a substratum or rather the source and invisible origin, without in itself being any form. With time, the Will also becomes aware of itself in these manifestations; it becomes aware that the world they show, albeit a world that it brought forth out of its own depths, is one of endless suffering and incurable misery, and can, if it so chooses, renounce itself, make an end by no longer producing any manifestations whatsoever. (Here the identity of the individual and the macrocosm plays a part: it is the individual primarily, who can renounce in this way, although Schopenhauer may mean to imply the macrocosm may do so too, perhaps simultaneously, in a kind of *Götterdämmerung*.) What is left is then the Naught, *das Nichts*. But, Schopenhauer adds, if we contemplate the lives of the saints (and mystics, he adds a little earlier) as art presents them to us, 'the gloomy impression of the Naught that hovers as a final goal behind all virtue and holiness, that we fear as children fear the dark, can be spirited away' not needing such myths as Brahma or Nirvana.

We admit freely, what remains after complete cessation of the Will is, it is true, for all who are still full of Will, Naught. But conversely, in those in whom the Will has turned and denied itself, this so real world of ours with all its suns and Milky Ways is – Naught. (*Die Welt*, etc. last paragraph)

As the dash indicates, the meaning of 'Naught' in the final sentence is not the same, presumably, as that in earlier uses of the word. It might almost suggest that such a profound insight restores the world to a state in which it is joyfully accepted (as Nietzsche proposed to do). But that can't be stated. As Wittgenstein, who was greatly influenced by Schopenhauer, put it, 'Whereof one cannot speak, thereof one must be silent' (*Tractatus* para.7). But it is through art, Schopenhauer maintains, that any communication of this kind is made. How is it then, when we contemplate Prospero's farewell to all the human condition?

> And like the baseless fabric of this vision,
> The cloud-capped towers, the gorgeous palaces,
> The solemn temples, the great globe itself,
> Yea, all which it inherit, shall dissolve
> And like this insubstantial pageant faded,
> Leave not a rack behind. We are such stuff
> As dreams are made on, and our little life
> Is rounded with a sleep.
> (*T* 4.1.148-158)

The beauty of these lines is itself an affirmation of what they deny; though what they deny is unsayable. Shakespeare and Schopenhauer come together not only in their chance agreement to speak of Will.

Nietzsche follows on after Schopenhauer in the sense that, where in Schopenhauer's thinking the Will denies itself, in Nietzsche it affirms itself, knowing itself fully to the extent that Schopenhauer's Will does, but pressing on in that full awareness. In the opening paragraphs of *Thus Spake Zarathustra* Nietzsche puts in a nutshell this aspect of his ideas: 'The Three Transformations' is a fable showing three phases, three confrontations of life. First comes the Camel, which like a conscience looks for the heaviest burdens it can carry; second is the Lion, the assertive roarer which affirms every aspect of its own existence, and lastly comes 'the wheel rolling by its own momentum [ein aus sich rollendes Rad]'. The wheel is burdened no longer by the self-knowledge that it has acquired or the need to confront the world with its nature: it spins on with an impetus derived solely from within itself.

The triadic pattern is clear. But despite the frequent allusions to Nietzsche in the works of G. Wilson Knight, I do not see that Nietzsche is more relevant to Shakespeare than any other writer in the dialectic tradition. Above all, he has little to say about love.

Ibsen, influenced here by Hegel or Hegelians, wrote before he began his 'social' plays three works that also form a triad. Peer Gynt is the would-be 'Emperor of Self'; Brand is his opposite, the extreme denier of

self; Julian the Apostate, in the unwieldy *Emperor and Galilean*, tries to
combine Dionysus and Christ, and fails. Shakespeare contrasts Troilus and
Cressida with Antony and Cleopatra, as whole plays, but never attempts
any such combinations as Ibsen does, or indeed as Nietzsche did when, at
the onset of insanity, he called himself 'the crucified Dionysus'. The
allusions in the Sonnets to both Christ and Eros cause no visible strain.

A late representative of the same tradition does, however, provide an
instance which leads to awareness of an aspect of the tradition hitherto not
mentioned. Thomas Mann was always inclined to divide society into two
general types, the bourgeois [Bürger] and the artist, the one practical, not
given to introspection, the other creative but, as Mann presents it, doomed.
This division leads on to his *Doktor Faustus*, a novel about a musical
composer, Leverkühn (Livebold), narrated by his conventionally-minded
friend, the good citizen Zeitblom. The novel is presented as a summation
of trends in German history which led to the disaster of Nazism, Leverkühn
being in several ways reminiscent of Nietzsche, and the musical
composition Zeitblom describes is a kind of symbol of those trends. It has
two movements. In each the sequence of notes is played in precisely the
same order, but in different keys, with different orchestration, different
tempi. In one the effect is of a tumultuous braying of Hell, shrieking
voices of agonised torment. In the other the effect is of glacial
smoothness, harmony, heavenly bliss. The suggestion is that a basic
sequence, like a ground bass, links the two totally different movements, as
though rendering some essential similarity between the two. Since this is
the creation of a man who has deliberately contracted a disease in order to
enliven his sluggish creativity, it is not clear how Mann intended it to be
regarded; however the analogy with the Sonnets is plain, though the
apparent scope of the symbolism goes far beyond any relationship between
a man and a woman.

As I have shown, in *Romeo and Juliet* and *A Midsummer Night's
Dream*, Shakespeare turns the story of Pyramus and Thisbe in two opposite
directions, in just the same way as Mann turns the sequence of notes.

When the Sonnets poet says of his lover that in him 'all il wel showes'
(40.13) he is saying in effect that what is bad in him both remains and is
yet good. The two aspects exist together rather as Leverkühn's two
musical movements share a common identity. Similarly the poet says of
his mistress 'thy blacke is fairest in my judgments place' (131.12). Yet he
can also dismiss that identity, separating the two aspects as in

I have sworne thee faire, and thought thee bright,
Who art as black as hell, as darke as night.
(147.13-14)

We do not know what the mistress has done to deserve this repudiation, nor do we know what the man has done. The vacillation reveals, however, a facet of the polarity-philosophy that has not shown up so far. In *Macbeth* the witches chant the words:

> Fair is foul and foul is fair;
> Hover through the fog and filthy air.
> (*Macbeth* 1.1.10)

They have a proverbial character, and are close to a phrase in Spenser's *Faerie Queene* 4.8.32: 'The faire grew foule, and foule grew faire in sight'. But they do not, as Knight maintained, state one of the main themes of the play, 'the reversal of values'.[8] Disturbingly, they say that, while bad can be improved on by showing it to be, or calling it good, good can also be shown to be or called bad. (As in Leverkühn's two movements, neither can claim pre-eminence. They simply exist alongside one another while sharing a suggested identity.)

The Sonnets poets' intention seems to be simply to praise what seems at first unworthy of praise. It is a lover's way of asserting his love despite impediments. Extending it to *Macbeth*, the paradox becomes much more questionable. It may be that Shakespeare became aware of this and renounced, if only temporarily, the dialectic philosophies. Others, however, continued them till quite recently.

In 1903 Stefan George, who translated the Sonnets into German, saw in Munich a 15-year old boy, Maximin, so handsome that he seemed the incarnation of beauty in a God. Out of the experience came the belief that a new elite of youth would renew civilization. The George-Kreis, a circle of friends, or rather disciples, seconded his efforts to do this by disciplined poetic beauty. The National Socialists tried to adopt George as a prophet, but he declined presidency of the Dichter-Akademie and went into exile.

C.G. Jung used alchemical texts in developing his psychological ideas, the *animus* and *anima* corresponding to the chemical opposites.

English literature has never adopted the dialectic as generally as German. Blake's *Marriage of Heaven and Hell*, partly derived, as he acknowledged from Boehme and Paracelsus, was not strictly a marriage. It was rather an affirmation of energy and libido: 'The lust of the goat is the bounty of God', without uniting this with any contrary. 'Energy is the only life and is from the body, and reason is the bound or outward circumference of energy. Energy is eternal delight'.[9] Reason, however, is

---

[8] *Macbeth*, Arden Edition, ed., K. Muir, 1959, pp.-5.
[9] *The Poems of William Blake*, ed. W.H. Stevenson, text by David V. Erdman, Longman 1971, p.106.

not a polar opposite of Energy. Despite Blake's saying, 'Without contraries is no progression',[10] 'Reason is for him merely a restraint on energy, increasingly weakening it if given the chance. 'Attraction and repulsion, reason and energy, love and hate, are necessary to human existence',[11] but these are not combined in any synthesis. 'Good is Heaven; Evil is Hell'.[12]

Both Rilke and Lawrence belong to a post-Nietzschean generation, and like him, they inherit the tradition of polar opposites. Both are much more concerned with love than he was. Rilke's *Sonnets to Orpheus* contrast with the Duino Elegies, as light to dark. In *Women in Love* Lawrence presents two pairs of characters, one bound for fulfilment, the other self-annihilating, parallel with Dionysus and Jesus, the would-be 'Salvator Mundi'. The nuances in both writers are many. I have tried to spell them out in *The German Tradition in Literature 1871-1945*.[13]

Equally close to the philosophy of coinciding opposites is T.S. Eliot. Not only does he quote Heraclitus in the epigraph to 'Burnt Norton'; his early study of Hegel coloured the rest of his thinking, as we see in *Murder in the Cathedral*. Here the chorus of women of Canterbury sing a version of the traditional *Benedicite omnia opera*, praising God for all things, but doing so in an entirely new way.

… all things affirm Thee in living; the bird in the air, both the hawk and the finch; the beast in the earth, both the wolf and the lamb; the worm in the soil and the worm in the belly.[14]

Whereas the psalm praises only the good, the women praise the hunters and the hunted, and the 'worm in the belly' suggests even malignant disease (a constantly troubling thought for Harry in *The Family Reunion*). All things exist only as seen by God, and that triumphantly includes even denial of God. The darkness declares his glory, not of being conquered, but in itself, by its own nature.

In 'Little Gidding' Eliot continues this line of thought in the fourth movement, taken by some readers to be about the experience of incendiaries falling on London in the Blitz of 1940.

The dove descending breaks the air
With flame of incandescent terror
Of which the tongues declare

---

[10] *op.cit* p.105.
[11] *loc.cit.*
[12] *loc.cit.*
[13] especially pp.340-349.
[14] *The Complete Poems and Plays of T.S. Eliot*, Faber 1969, p.281.

The one discharge from sin and error.
The only hope, or else despair
    Lies in the choice of pyre or pyre –
    To be redeemed from fire by fire.[15]

The dove is the dove of the Pentecost, raining down flames of fire on each of the disciples' heads and enabling them to 'speak with tongues'. It can also be seen as the hundreds of fire-bombs dropped by German bombers, purely evil and destruction in intent. Their message is, however, to understand the choice all must make: to choose to be consumed by fire of love or to suffer death by literal burning. It is Love, the poem continues, that has created the 'intolerable shirt of flame' from which there is no escape. Love acts in a way indistinguishable, to all appearances, from hatred. The incendiaries are brought by the dove itself.

There are passages in Shakespeare – particularly on the death of Desdemona, where an analogy can be made even with this hard to accept paradox. It would be good if one could point to yet another parallel between the two poets. But when Eliot writes, quoting Julian(a) of Norwich:

And all shall be well
And all manner of thing shall be well
When the tongues of flame are in-folded
Into the crowned knot of fire
And the fire and the rose are one.[16]

he looks to a future condition, of which perhaps a glimpse can be had now – 'Quick now, here, now always', but which can only really be beyond time and experience. Shakespeare in the Sonnets would like to believe in a comparable union of opposites, but the future remains for him out of reach. It is perhaps for this reason that his plays gradually lose the ambiguities that they had at first, and finally shun them altogether, albeit with sympathy.

We should perhaps look again at Sonnet 117, quoted earlier. There can be little doubt, as I have argued, that the 'great deserts' the poet has failed to repay are Christ's, or that the 'deare purchas'd right' (117.2 and 6) is the one spoken of by St Paul. The poet has 'hoysted saile to al the windes' (117.7), and now looks back with misgivings. His defence, that he meant always to 'proove [prove rather than test]' the constancy and virtue of the lover's love, sounds improbable. But Shakespeare may very well, like

---

[15] *op.cit.* p.196.
[16] *op.cit.* p.198.

Chaucer, have felt the need to cover himself from a Jesus who could shoot
at him in his 'wakened hate'. Chaucer confessed in the final words of *The
Canterbury Tales* that along with many another book 'and many a song
and many a leccherous lay' he must beg for mercy. In Shakespeare's time
Christianity was less uniformly imposed. Marlowe could be called an
atheist, but Jonson returned to his Catholic faith, and Donne gave up his
erotic poems; he even wrote some of the Holy Sonnets with Shakespeare's
in mind, giving them a purely spiritual meaning. In 1595 Southwell faced
torture and gruesome execution for his steadfast faith. There was little
encouragement in society at large to go one's own way in religious matters.
So it is understandable that Sonnet 117 renounces the speculative thoughts
that inspired so many other Sonnets and that *The Tempest*, while
sympathising with the philosophies of contradiction, goes on without them.
It does not necessarily indicate a permanent change of mind. It may have
been, as so many other Sonnets were, the expression of a momentary
mood, another contradiction, this time contrasting with the tenor of the
remainder. On that point we can have no certainty. Does *Timon of Athens*
imply Shakespeare's own awareness that disinterested generosity can have
no influence on other men, who remain as selfish as ever they were; that
the stone, so to speak, does not transmute others? Perhaps after all he
preferred to remember that his 'oblation' was one of 'mutuall render, onely
me for thee' (125.12), and that the phoenix and turtle fled from hence in a
mutual flame.

EPILOGUE

DANTE AND SHAKESPEARE

'Shakespeare gives the greatest *width* of human passion; Dante the greatest altitude and greatest depth. They complement each other.' T.S. Eliot's comparison[1] makes sense; he is speaking of the '*entire* dramatic work', contrasted with the *Divine Comedy*. You could wish Eliot had had more to say about 'the comparison of the *Vita Nuova* with the Sonnets, than that it is 'another, and interesting occupation', since he follows this with 'Dante and Shakespeare divide the modern [scil. Western] world between them; there is no third'.[2] If we take into account the Sonnets on universal love, which compare well with those in the *Vita Nuova*, we reach a point where we can add to Shakespeare's achievement at least as much altitude as Dante's, and as much depth.

In some ways the thought of the two poets can be seen as corresponding to the stricter aspects of Christianity, associated with the Old Testament, and the more liberal aspects, associated with mercy. They also correspond broadly to medieval Christianity and the expansion that came with the Renaissance.

Dante concludes the *Paradiso* with the words:

All'alta fantasia qui mancò possa;
  ma già volgeva il mio disiro e il *velle*
  sì come rota ch'egualmenté è mossa,
L'amor che move il sole e l'altre stelle.

To the high fantasy here power failed; but already my desire and will were rolled – even as a wheel that moveth equally – by the Love that moves the sun and the other stars.

He has just written

---

[1] T.S. Eliot, *Selected Essays*, Faber, Third Enlarged Edition 1951, p.265.
[2] p.265.

O luce eternal, che sola in te sidi,
    sola t'intendi, e, da te intelletta
    ed intendente te, ami ed arridi!

O Light eternal who only in thyself abidest, only thyself dost understand,
and to thyself, self-understood, self-understanding, turnest love and
smiling!
(*Paradiso* XXXIII, 124-6)

This is close to Plato's vision of universal love, and to the same love
expressed in Sonnet 124, that 'all alone stands hugely pollitick' and is
'buylded far from accident' (124.11-12). We may say, while
acknowledging that Dante is most unlikely to have known the *Symposium*,
(still to be a revelation in the fifteenth century), that both he and
Shakespeare are attracted to the same source, however transmitted and
transmuted over many years. The works connected with if not inspired by
this vision are, however, farther apart than one might have thought
possible. They are parts of the great surge of ideas of Love over many
centuries.

Dante's Hell offers no hope of return to any who enter it, as in Jesus'
parable of the rich man and the beggar where the rich man in intolerable
heat is denied even a sip of water. For the Sonnets poet his mistress is 'as
black as hell' (147.14) but no such hell is meant as Dante portrays. The
Sonnets poet does not see his condemnation of the mistress as inevitable:
it is rather a test of his ability to love despite impediments that he sees her
in such drastic terms. Dante feels no compunction, though he may
sympathize with some of the sufferers, and on seeing Paolo and Francesca
whirled about in each others' arms he 'fell, as a dead body falls' (e caddi,
come corpo morto cade, *Inferno* V 142). He may be thinking of how
closely he has come to sharing their fate. But in the main he is content to
accept what divine justice has ordained, which provides for some sinners
the possibility of being purged of their sins and so ascending to the higher
level.

At the highest level Dante is blessed with a vision of Beatrice, praying
for him to the Virgin Mary, whose prayers for humanity show him the
nature of divine mercy. It is a moment entirely without any hint of erotic
love. Here Shakespeare differs most of all from Dante. In Sonnets 135
and 136 the confusion between himself, or rather the Sonnets poet, and the
poet's mistress is so great, and the sexual meanings of 'Will' are so
pervasive, that he appears, even though in a less than serious mood, to
have more in common with Oriental religion. In the plays, sexuality is
simply human, but it extends from crude bawdy to impassioned devotion.

His embrace of the whole of human experience, never quite complete, marks him off from Dante more clearly than anything.

The Sonnets poet, like Drake and Magellan, has 'hoysted saile to all the windes' (117.7). Where Dante relies on Aristotle and Aquinas, and offers a comprehensive picture of the world as seen in his time by men of learning, while still remaining orthodox, Shakespeare turns to the world of Plato, Paracelsus, Castiglione, Cusanus, Bruno, and Boccaccio. He alludes to Christ in the Sonnets, though scarcely ever in the plays (except the medieval histories). He contrasts Christian charity with the commonly accepted view of Jewish rigour, but puts in the Jew's mouth an unparalleled defence of human equality, and allows Falstaff to defend himself with 'Banish plump Jack and banish all the world' (H4.2.4.26), while bringing Richard III and Iago, Macbeth and Goneril to a just condemnation. The many ambiguities of the Sonnets would have displeased Dante, who could never have written 'Lascivious grace, in whom all il wel showes' (40.13), nor could Shakespeare have condemned to eternal torment so many of his contemporaries in the real world, as Dante does.

Shakespeare claims no authority for what he writes; though he allows characters like Antony and Brutus to be described in extravagant quasi-godlike terms, and even grants himself or his poetic persona universal pre-eminence., this is always with an ambiguous qualification. He knows he exaggerates yet simultaneously affirms. Dante is in tune with Church doctrine all the time – purgatory had only been officially validated not long before he wrote. Shakespeare is writing poetry, not theology, and poetry may be feigning. This gives a different standing to all his work. It is a fiction that can persuade.

Dante writes in a verse-form of his own invention, *terza rima*, requiring triple rhymes continually interlocking with other triple rhymes. Though rhymes are more easily found in Italian than in English, great discipline is required to maintain such a form throughout. The sonnets of *La Vita Nuova* are similarly difficult in form: ABBA ABBA CDE CDE, again requiring many rhymes. Shakespeare's are simply three quatrains, rhyming separately, and a couplet. Blank verse is the easiest to compose, the least constricting. The *Divine Comedy* has 100 cantos, each of three sections having 33 cantos, except that the Inferno has an additional one. The plays are often divided into five acts not by Shakespeare but by Pope; they disregard the three unities of time, space and subject-matter. The Sonnets are said to be divided into two sections, before and after Sonnet 126, the first containing Sonnets about or addressed to a man, the second Sonnets about or addressed to a woman, but this takes no account of several Sonnets not addressed to either sex. Apart from Sonnets 1-17 there is no structure. The young man is addressed as though he were of dual sex, and both he and the mistress have features in common.

Dante's whole work, he said, was undertaken 'not for a speculative but for a practical end' and his purpose was, in the *Comedy*, and expressly in the *Paradiso* to 'remove those who are living in this life from the state of wretchedness, and to lead them to the state of blessedness'.[3] This is poetry at the service of the Church, reinforcing and illustrating its teachings in the same way as did the *Biblia Pauperum*. The aim is supported and given missionary capacity by the *Lecturae Dantis* in which, in Italy and elsewhere, scholars lecture on a single canto in a series eventually treating them all, each time ending with the pleasure of hearing a recital of the canto in question. This is a continuing basis for its popular success. Shakespeare aims in his plays at entertaining an audience involving all ranks of society, bearing witness to a common humanity, a sense of justice and sometimes of patriotism. To pursue the comparison with Christianity, he represents a kind of 'broad church', such as is said to be found in the Church of England. As for that Church, globalization has brought difficulties. Where the Archbishop of Canterbury is faced with reconciling African Christians taught by fundamentalist missionaries of the nineteenth and twentieth centuries with the liberal tendencies said by some to be represented by bishops who are atheists, so Shakespearean performances have been presented in ways far removed from the traditional. It is not merely that there have, laudably, been a Zulu *Macbeth* and a Japanese *Lear* whose daughters had to become sons, since in medieval Japan daughters could not inherit, nor is it that *The Tempest* is not about colonialism or *Julius Caesar* about Fascism. Hamlet is not another Oedipus; rather it is that directors feel obliged to present some original interpretations, however unlikely, in order to draw an audience away from so many alternative presentations. Nor is it that Shakespearean language becomes in some plays more and more difficult to understand. The English language itself is becoming more and more leaderless, whereas medieval Latin, reflected in Dante's Italian, remains unchanged and internationally authoritative, though not now universal. We do not, in the Western world, want a theatre like the old Chinese, where connoisseurs judged a performance by its ability to adhere to traditional ways of acting, yet there are still producers like Greg Doran, who remain both original and traditional.

---

[3] Epist. and Can. Grands. 273-275 and 267-270 (§§ 16 and 15) quoted in the Temple Classics edition, *The Paradiso of Dante Alighieri*, Dent, London 1930, p.409.

Eliot's comparison invites as to think again, not much less than a century later, about the extent to which Shakespeare and Dante still complement each other. One could put it like this: Dante as a poet stands for tradition, formal structure, adherence to a Christian belief that is maintained unchanged today by the Roman Catholic Church, whose millions of believers will always be ready to acknowledge the Pope, even while contemplating some departures in the Church from its ancient role. His vision like theirs, is of a world united in faith under a sole ruler, a universal love maintained through authority. Shakespeare's is a more fluid world, owning no single authority, using no such strict forms as Dante uses. His ability to feel sympathy with a wide range of human emotions and human characters could be valuable in a globalized world where such wide understanding is going to be essential. Notable in Shakespeare is both his common touch, his straightforward good sense, of the kind shown by Emilia, when she denounces Othello for his sheer folly, but also in his ability to undermine at the same time as he affirms. The coincidence of opposites allows him both to affirm himself to the uttermost and at the same time to deny his own powers, whether as a poet or as a lover. He is completely unsystematic, even in making use of the dialectical philosophy, and can discard it at all, as he does in *The Tempest*, or not even contemplate it, as in the histories. This makes him all the more difficult to comprehend. Others 'abide our question'. Even when we are able to follow him into the most difficult aspects of his mind, he still remains free of our expectations.

BIBLIOGRAPHY

Aristotle, *Aristotle's Metaphysics*, tr. John Warrington, intro. by Sir Davis Ross, Dent, London 1956.

Auden, W.H., 'Introduction to the Sonnets' in Barnet, 1952, pp.1722-29.

Audi, Robert (ed.), *The Cambridge Dictionary of Philosophy*, 2nd edn, Cambridge University Press, Cambridge 2005.

Baldwin, Anne and Hatton, Sarah (edd.), *Platonism and the English Imagination*, Cambridge University Press, Cambridge 1994. (Stephen Medcalf, 'Shakespeare on beauty, truth and transcendence', and John Roe, 'Italian Neoplatonism and the Poetry of Sidney, Shakespeare and Donne'.)

Baldwin, T.W., *On the Literary Genetics of Shakespeare's Poems and Sonnets*, Illinois 1950.

Barker, Simon (ed.), New Casebooks, *Shakespeare's Problem Plays. All's Well That Ends Well, Measure for Measure, Troilus and Cressida*, Palgrave Macmillan Houndmills, Basingstoke, Hampshire and 175 Fifth Avenue, New York 2005.

Barnet, Sylvan (ed.), *The Signet Classic Edition of Shakespeare's Works*, Harcourt Brace Jovanovich, New York 1963.

Berman, Sandra, 'The Sonnet Over Time: A Study in the Sonnets of Petrarch, Shakespeare and Baudelaire', University of North Carolina, *Studies in Comparative Literature*, 1988.

Booth, Stephen (ed.), *Shakespeare's Sonnets*, Yale University Press, New Haven 1977.

Brinton, H.H., *The Mystic Will* (based on a study of the philosophy of Jacob Boehme), London 1931.

Burke, Peter, 'The Fortunes of the Courtier' in *The European Reception of Castiglione's Cortegiano*, Polity Press, Cambridge 1995.

Burrow, Colin (ed.), The Oxford Shakespeare. *The Complete Sonnets and Poems*, Oxford University Press, Oxford 2002.
'Why Shakespeare is not Michelanglo' in *Thinking with Shakespeare, Comparative and Interdisciplinary Essays* for A.D. Nuttall, edd. William Poole and Richard Scholar, 2007.

Castiglione, Balthasar, *The Book of the Courtier*, transl. Sir Thomas Hoby. Intro. J.H. Whitfield, Everyman's Library, Dent, London 1974.

Chambers, R.W., 'Man's Unconquerable Mind', London, Jonathan Cape 1952, reproduced in *Measure for Measure*, Signet Classic, no date.

Cobb, Noel, *Prospero's Island, The Secret Alchemy at the Heart of* The Tempest, Coventure, London 1984.

Coleridge, Samuel Taylor, *Coleridge's Essays and Lectures on Shakespeare and Some Other Old Poets and Dramatists*, Everyman's Library, Dent, London, no date.

Croll, Oswald, *Philosophy Reformed and Improved ... The Mysteries of Nature* by Osw. Croll ... *The Mysteries of the Creation by Paracelsus*, transl. H. Pinnell, London 1657, p.214.

Danby, John F. '*Antony and Cleopatra*: A Shakespearean Adjustment' in *Elizabethan and Jacobean Tragedy Studies in Sidney, Shakespeare, Beaumont and Fletcher*, Faber, London 1952.

Dee, John, *Essential Readings*, ed. and intro. Gerald Suster, Crucible 1980.

Delcourt, Maria, *Hermaphrodite. Myths and Rites of the Bisexual Figure in Classical Antiquity*, transl. from the French by Jennifer Nicholson, Studio Books, London 1961.

Dobbs, Betty Jo Tetter, The Foundations of Newton's Alchemy or 'The Hunting of the Greene Lyon', Cambridge University Press, Cambridge 1975.

Duncan-Jones, Katherine (ed.), The Arden Shakespeare, third series, *Shakespeare's Sonnets*, London 1997.

Duveen, D.I. *Bibliotheca Alchemica et Chemica. An Annotated Catalogue of Printed Books on Alchemy, Chemistry, and Cognate Subjects in the Library of Denis I. Duveen*, London 1949.

Eliot, T.S., *The Complete Poems and Plays*, Faber, London 1969.

Empson, William, *Seven Types of Ambiguity*.

Erne, Lukas, *Shakespeare a Literary Dramatist*, Cambridge University Press, Cambridge 2005.

Evans, G. Blakemore, The New Cambridge Shakespeare. *The Sonnets*. Intro., Anthony Hecht, Cambridge University Press, Cambridge 1996.

Ferguson, J., *Bibliotheca Chemica. A Catalogue of the Alchemical, Chemical and Pharmaceutical Books in the Collection of the late James Young of Kelly and Durris*, 2 vols., Glasgow 1906.

—. *Catalogue of the Ferguson Collection of Books, Mainly Relating to Alchemy, Chemistry, Witchcraft and Gypsies*, 2 vols., Glasgow 1943.

Festugière, A.J., *La Révélation d'Hermès Trismégiste*, vol. I, 'L'Astrologie et les sciences occultes', *Études bibliques*, Lecoffre, Paris 1944.

Fineman, Joel, *Shakespeare's Perjured Eye: the invention of poetic subjectivity in the Sonnets*, University of California Press, Berkeley, Los Angeles, London 1986.

Fludd, R., *Philosophia Moysaica*, Govdae 1638.

Gardiner, Patrick, *Schopenhauer*, Penguin, Harmondsworth 1963.

Gratarolus, G. (ed.), *Verae alchemiae ... doctrina*, Basileae 1561.

Gray, Ronald D., *Goethe the Alchemist. A Study of Alchemical Symbols in Goethe's Literary and Scientific Works*, Cambridge University Press, Cambridge 1952.

—. 'Will in the Universe', Shakespeare's Sonnets, Plato's *Symposium*, alchemy and Renaissance Neoplatonism, in *Shakespeare Survey* 59, pp.225-238, Cambridge University Press 2006.

—. *Brecht the Dramatist*, Cambridge University Press, Cambridge 1973.

—. *Ibsen, a Dissenting View*, Cambridge University Press, Cambridge 1977.

—. 'A Dissenting View of Ibsen' in *Proceedings, VII International Ibsen Conference, Grimstad 1993*, Centre for Ibsen Studies, Oslo 1994.

Greenblatt, Stephen, *Will in the World. How Shakespeare Became Shakespeare*, Jonathan Cape, London 2004.

Gross, John, *Shylock, Four Hundred Years in the Life of a Legend*, Vintage, London 1994.

Grudin, Robert, *Mighty Opposites. Shakespeare and Renaissance Contrariety*, University of California Press 1979.

Happold, F.C., *Mysticism. A Study and an Anthology*, Penguin, Harmondsworth 1963.

Healy, Margaret, *Shakespeare, Alchemy, and the Creative Imagination, The Sonnets and 'A Lover's Complaint'*. Announced for 2011 by Cambridge University Press.

Helmont, J.V. van, *A Ternary of Paradoxes*, London 1650.

Hopkins, A.J., *Alchemy, Child of Greek Philosophy*, Columbia University Press, New York 1934.

Howald, Ernst, *Die Anfänge der abendländischen Philosophie*. Trans. by Michael Grünwald, Artemis, Zürich 1949.

Hughes, E.R., *Chinese Philosophy in Classical Times*, Dent, London 1942.

Huxley, Aldous, *The Perennial Philosophy*, Faber, London 1946.

Inge, W.R., *Christian Mysticism*, London 1899.

Ingram, W.C., and Redpath, Theodore, (edd.), *Shakespeare's Sonnets*, Hodder and Stoughton, London 1978.

Jackson, MacDonald P., *Shakespeare's 'A Lover's Complaint': Its Date and Authenticity*, Auckland, New Zealand 1965.

—. 'A Lover's Complaint Revisited', *Shakespeare Studies*, 32, 267-94, 2004.

Jayne, Sears, *Plato in Renaissance England*, Kluwer Academic Publishers, Dordrecht, Boston, London 1995.

Jung, C.G., *Psychologie und Alchemie*, Zürich 1944.

—. *Die Erlösungsvorstellungen in der Alchemie*, Zürich 1937.

—. *Die Psychologie der Übertragung, Erläutert anhand einer alchemistischen Bilderserie*, Zürich 1946.

—. *The Secret of the Golden Flower* (trans. R. Wilhelm, commentary by C.G. Jung), London 1945. (A Chinese work on alchemy which throws much light on Western doctrines.)

Kermode, Frank, *Shakespeare's Language*, Allen Lane, The Penguin Press, London 2000.

Kerrigan, John (ed.), The New Penguin Shakespeare. *'The Sonnets; and 'A Lover's Complaint*, 1986.

Khunrath, H., Vom hylealischen … Chaos, der Naturgemässen Alchymie und Alchemisten, Frankfurt, 1707, reprint. (Follower of Ripley)

Kirk, G.S. and Raven, J.E. *The Presocratic Philosophers. A Critical History with a Selection of the Texts*, Cambridge 1969.

Knight, G. Wilson, *The Wheel of Fire. Interpretations of Shakespearean Tragedy with Three New Essays*, Methuen, London 1949.
The Mutual Flame, Methuen, London.

Knox Poole, C., *The Works of Shakespeare, The Sonnets*. The Arden Shakespeare, 3rd edn., revised 1943.

Landry, Hilton (ed.) *New Essays on Shakespeare's Sonnets*, AMS Press Inc., New York 1976.

Leishman, J.B., *Themes and Variations in Shakespeare's Sonnets*, Hutchinson, London, 2nd edn. 1963.

Leuba, J.H., *The Psychology of Religious Mysticism*, London 1925.

Levin, Harry, Introduction to *The Comedy of Errors* in Barnet, p.77.

Mackail, J.W., 'A Lover's Complaint', *Essays and Studies*, 3, 51-70, 1912.

McCanles, Michael, *Dialectical Criticism and Renaissance Literature*, University of California Press, Berkeley, Los Angeles and London 1975.

McLean, Adam, Alchemy Web Bookshop (alchemy@dialpipex.com).

Mahood, M.M., *Shakespeare's Word-Play*, Methuen, London 1957.

Maier, Michael, *Viatorium, hoc est de montibus planetarum septem, seu metallorum*, Oppenheim 1618.

Martindale, Charles, 'Shakespeare Philosopher' in Poole, William and Scholar, Richard.

Martindale, C. and M., *Shakespeare and the Uses of Antiquity*, London and New York 1990.

Maxwell, J.C. (ed.), *The Poems*, The Cambridge Shakespeare, 1960.
The New Shakespeare, *The Poems*, Cambridge University Press, Cambridge 1966.

Montaigne, *Essais*, ed. Albert Thibaudet, Editions de la Pléiade, Livre III, Chapitre V, 'Sur des Vers de Virgile', Paris 1933.

Muir, Kenneth, "'A Lover's Complaint": A Reconsideration', chapter 12 in *Shakespeare the Professional and Related Studies*, Heinemann, London 1973, pp.204-219.
—. *Shakespeare's Sonnets*, George Allen and Unwin, London 1979.
Nicoll, Charles, *The Chemical Theatre*, 1980.
Nuttall, A.D., *Shakespeare the Thinker*, Yale University Press, New Haven and London 2007.
—. 'Shakespeare and the Idea of Love' in *Two Concepts of Allegory. A Study of Shakespeare and the Logic of Allegorical Expression*, London 1967, pp.108-131.
Paolucci, Anne and Henry (ed.), *Hegel on Tragedy*, Doubleday and Co. Inc. Garden City, New York1962.
Paracelsus, *Opera Omnia*, Genevae 1658.
—. *Hermetic and Alchemical Writings*, edited by A.E. Waite, London 1894.
Partridge, Eric, *Shakespeare's Bawdy. A Literary and Psychological Essay and a Comprehensive Glossary*, Revised 1968, Routledge, London.
Plato, 'The Symposium' in *Five Dialogues of Plato*, trans. Michael Joyce, Everyman Library, Dent, London 1938.
Platt, Peter G., *Shakespeare and the Culture of Paradox*, 2009.
Plotinus, *Select Works of Plotinus: Thomas Taylor's Translation*, ed. G.R.S. Mead, Bell, London 1914.
Poole, William and Scholar, Richard, *Thinking with Shakespeare. Comparative and Inter-disciplinary Essays for A.D. Nuttall*, Modern Humanities Research Association 2007.
Read, J., *Prelude to Chemistry, an outline of alchemy, its literature and relationships*, George Bell and Sons Ltd, London 1936.
Redgrove, H.S., *Alchemy, Ancient and Modern*, London 1911.
    Bygone Beliefs, London 1920. (Ch. ix: 'The Quest of the Philosophers' Stone'. Ch. x: The Phallic Element in Alchemy'.)
Ridley, M.R. *Keats' Craftsmanship. A Study in Poetic Development*, Methuen, London 1963.
Ripley, George, *The Compound of Alchemy*, 1591.
    The Mirror of Alchemy, 1597.
Roe, John (ed.), The New Cambridge Shakespeare. *The Poems*, Cambridge 1992.
Rollins, Hyder Edward (ed.), *A New Variorum Edition of Shakespeare. Poems*, Philadelphia 1938.
—. (ed.), *A New Variorum Edition of Shakespeare. Sonnets*, J.B. Lippincott Company, Philadelphia and London 1938.

Saslow, James M., 'Michelangelo: Sculpture, Sex and Gender' in Sarah Blake McHam (ed.), *Looking at Italian Renaissance Sculpture*, Cambridge University Press, Cambridge 1998.

Schalkwyk, David, *Speech and Performance in Shakespeare's Sonnets and Plays*, Cambridge University Press, Cambridge 2003.

Shakespeare, Love and Service, Cambridge, Cambridge University Press 2007.

Schiffer, James (ed.), *Shakespeare's Sonnets. Critical Essays*, Garland Publishing Inc, A Member of the Taylor and Francis Group, New York and London 2000.

Schmitt, Charles B. (ed.), *The Cambridge History of Renaissance Philosophy* (eds. Quentin Skinner, Eckhard Kessler, asst.ed. Jill Kraye), Cambridge University Press, Cambridge 1988.

Schoenfeldt, Michael (ed.), *A Companion to Shakespeare's Sonnets*, Blackwell Publishing Books, Oxford 2006.

Silberer, H., *Probleme der Mystik und ihrer Symbolik*, Leipzig und Wien 1914. (A Freudian study of alchemy.)

Starkie, Enid, *Baudelaire*. Chapter 4, *La Vénus Noire*, pp.69-81, Victor Gollancz, London, n.d. (1933).

Starkey, G. (Eirenaeus Philalethes*), Ripley Reviv'd*, London 1678.

Secrets Reveal'd, London 1669.

—. *Enarratio methodica trium Gebri medicinarum in quibus continetur Lapidis Philosophica vera confectio*, London 1678.

Taylor, Charles, *Hegel*, Cambridge University Press, Cambridge 1975.

Taylor, F. Sherwood (ed.), *Ambix* (being the Journal of the Society for the Study of Alchemy and Early Chemistry, London), vol. I, 1938, vols. II and III, 1938-49, vol. IV, 1949.

Underhill, E. (John Cordelier), *Mysticism. A Study in the nature and development of man's spiritual consciousness*, London 1911.

Valentine, Basil, *Von dem grossen Stein der Uhralten*, Franckenhausen 1602.

—. *De occulta philosophia*, Leipzig 1603.

—. *Von den natürlichen und übernatürlichen Dingen,* Leipzig 1603.

—. *Offenbarung der verborgenen Handgriffe auf das Universal gerichtet*, Erffurt 1624.

Vendler, Helen, *The Art of Shakespeare's Sonnets*, The Belknap Press of Harvard University Press, Cambridge, Mass. and London 1997.

Vickers, Brian, *Shakespeare, 'A Lover's Complaint' and John Davies of Hereford*, Cambridge University Press, Cambridge 2007.

Wells, Stanley (ed. and intro.), *'Shakespeare's Sonnets' and 'A Lover's Complaint'*, Oxford University Press, Oxford 1985.

Wells, Stanley and Taylor, Gary (edd.), Shakespeare's *The Complete Works*, Oxford University Press, Oxford 1986.

Wilson, J. Dover, The New Shakespeare, *The Sonnets*, Cambridge University Press, Cambridge 1966.

—. *What Happened in 'Hamlet'*, Cambridge University Press, Cambridge 1935.

Yates, Frances, *A Study of Love's Labour's Lost*, Cambridge University Press, Cambridge 1936.

—. *Giordano Bruno and the Hermetic Tradition*, Routledge and Kegan Paul 1964.

—. *Giordano Bruno and the Hermetic Tradition, The Rosicrucian Enlightenment*, 1972.

—. *The Occult Philosophy in the Elizabethan Age*, Routledge and Kegan Paul, London 1979.

—. *Lull and Bruno. Collected Essays. Vol. 1*, Routledge and Kegan Paul, London 1982.

—. *Shakespeare's Last Plays. A New Approach*, Routledge and Kegan Paul, London 2007.

Zaehner, R.C., *Mysticism Sacred and Profane*, 1967.

Zolla, Élémire, *The Androgyne, Fusion of the Sexes*, Thames and Hudson, London 1981.

INDEX